WIN PUBLISHING

I BELIEVE
IN ANGELS

"You have to be willing to risk to fly with the angels."

by Jerri Curry, Ph.D. MFCC

illustrated by Ron Short
book design and production by Susan Pinkerton

This book is dedicated to Danny.

"G.G., thanks for reading me some of the book you are writing. I like it. I did say the things you told everybody. I like talking to you and I tell my friends what we talk about".

I respond, "I also tell my friends, Danny."

"What we talk about is true, G.G.".

"I know, Danny."

"G.G., I miss God. I don't see God anymore, but I will again, someday. Did you know my family is the whole world?"

"Yes, Danny, I write about that in the book, too".

Danny Camacho, six-year-old-grandson to Jerri Curry

To order book, send $14.00 plus tax and shipping to:
Win Publishing
936-B Seventh Street, #110, Novato, California 94945 USA
(707) 428-0228

Printed in the United States of America
10 9 8 7 6 5 4 3 2
Library of Congress Catalog Card Number 95-90358
ISBN: 0-944586-09-0

Acknowledgments

I have learned that the challenge in life is how to handle separation with ease and dignity, so I can experience wholeness in every part of who I am and what I do. I am aware that synchronicity has brought many people in to my life. Some have stayed while others have taken different paths. I wish all people who have touched me, either as a loving friend or as a tyrannical teacher, blessings of abundance, joy and recognition.

My spiritual sisters and closest confidants are Diane Copitzky and Beverly Chinello and their support has been a constant. I am also blessed to have my daughter, Kathleen, her husband David, and their family in my life. My grandsons, Danny who is six-years-old and Chad who is one-year-old, are my teachers and I cherish these connections. My mother, Jennie and my step-father, Harry, have shared many moments of laughter and love with me. My aunt Virginia and aunt Louise and their family members are lights in my life and I love spending time with them. I appreciate Claudia Miles and her editing insights and consistent words of support for this book and for me. I deeply appreciate all of you and I love you with all the love I have to give in life.

Others who have crossed my path in meaningful moments are Katherine Bayh, Ann Beasley, Barbara Rose Billings, Marcial Boo, John Brodie, J. Niley Dorit, John Eger, Jeff Francheschi, Leigh Gaitskill, Deborah Grandinetti, Helen Jacobsen, Marge Katsantones, J.P. Lama, Candy Lightner, Father John Lo Schiavo, Jane Lowe, Michele of Bangkok, Tom and Lindsay Martin, Drew Mazer, Ruth McIssac, George and Linda McLaird, Bobbie Monnette, Ed Nucci, Sharon Olson, Charles Ramey, Bob Rausch, Heather Reed, Amy Richards, Santi, Michael Schmidt, Barbara and Terry Schukart, Joy

Kircher, Murray and Pat Sobel, Joan Stafford, Josephine Taylor, Ellen Thomas, Sharon Valentine, William Walsh, and Jim and Stephanie Wills. Thank you for sharing the moments even if sometimes that may have seemed difficult to do.

To my clients. I cannot name you individually but you know who you are. I give you my admiration and respect. I have experienced your Light and it shines brightly in our world.

There are people I have met in the child victim field. Some friends I have made include David Corwin, Jim Coughlin, Karen French, Seth Goldstein, Dick Gordy, Bill Hammond, Georgia Hilgeman, Laurie Lindenbaum, David Lloyd, Dan Lobovitz, Dave Paulson, Jim Petty, Senator Bob Presley, and Ron Stephens. You are the beacons of light to the children of our nation and I am proud to be called your colleague.

Ron Short is the artist who spent many hours of creative inspiration in providing the artwork in this book. His talent is obvious and his gift deeply appreciated. Ron Short Designs Office is located in Salt Lake City, Utah. He has been widely aclaimed in Russia and he is becoming more recognized and honored in his own Country, the United States. Thank you for your gift, Ron and for the reflection of beauty you bring to this book.

Susan Pinkerton: we continue our work, and it has been an experience of connection I cherish. As the producer of this book, particularly in a last minute flurry of deadlines, and the angels playing with its' production, your talent and staying centered is a significant hallmark of who you are. Thank you for the gifts you so freely share, and the laughs we have had together.

The sherpas taught me to share my vulnerability and to learn how to receive nurturing and compassion. The sherpas of the Himalayas, which include Sherap Tenzing-Sherpa, Nima Wangchuk, Tek Bhadur, Harka Bhadur and Man Bhadur and

Dorjee, are the strongest, most loving men I have had the privilege of knowing. You have my deepest respect, love and gratitude. Thank you for sharing your Light with me and for saving my life.

For those of you whom I have not had the privilege of meeting consciously, but who are destined to be in my life, I look with anticipation to those relationships, and I will appreciate the opportunity to practice what I have learned in life.

ABOUT THE AUTHOR

Jerri Curry is a nationally recognized advocate for child victims and a licensed marriage and family therapist, who holds a Ph.D. in clinical psychology. She also serves as a superior court mediator and forensic consultant for government agencies. But that's not all of her; there's another part, too — a deeply aware and mystical part capable of seeing through the veil of reality to the wondrous connection between all living things.

TABLE OF CONTENTS

INTRODUCTION

I Believe in Angels is my story. It is about choices in life and free will. I never thought I had many choices as I lived my life; now I know I have all the choices I could ever want and that I can make those choices freely. Victims are people who don't think they have choices, but they do. I know, because I was a victim for many years but that has changed. I live my life with ease and there are few struggles.

My story is also about synchronicity. That word may sound vague but it is really a very simple concept; like ripples in a pond, one reaching out touching the other. It is the simultaneous interconnection of all living things. The universe was created by synchronicity. It is through that concept that I now understand the lessons of separation and connection. My success in learning to experience separation with dignity has allowed me to feel complete connection and it leads me toward my individual, community and worldly wholeness.

Given my background, it is ironic that I've come to believe life does not have to be a struggle. I experienced domestic violence in one relationship, and the betrayal of extramarital affairs in another. At sixteen, my daughter was in a near-fatal car accident, resulting in a coma, and not expected to live. I was also the victim of two vehicle accidents. One was a head-on collision; and the other was as a pedestrian in a busy city crosswalk hit by a bus going twenty-five miles per hour that threw me twenty feet in the air. I've been the target of a sexual assault and a rape in my lifetime. I could go on, but I think my point is made! I have also had incredible spiritual experiences that placed me in a state of grace with God's direct guidance. I have been blessed and strengthened from all my life's experiences even though I would have preferred not to have several of them, but those events occurred when I felt I had to struggle through life.

The knowledge of learning how to live with ease came in the near death struggle I had while climbing near Mt. Everest. It also came from my personal connection with His Holiness, the high Lama of Nepal, in the Tengboche Monastery on Christmas day 1993. My story is told within the framework of that trekking experience but it is just as much about my spiritual journey throughout my life.

They don't tell us when we are children that life may not be easy. If, at an early age, I had been taught to consider **choices** that might have been available to me, perhaps life would have been easier. However, life threatening asthmatic attacks and pneumonia left me little choice but to be placed frequently in the hands of doctors, and separation from my parents gave me the knowledge that separation is the hardest lesson in life. Nothing is harder. There are many forms of separation, but each experience is, at best, challenging and, at worst, devastating. My separation issues as a child may have been similar to what many children experience during their childhood. Other children will often get the full impact of separation even before they can crawl. I'm writing this book for the children, too.

We usually learn through our moments of pain, and sometimes, through joy. I know I have. Throughout my story, I want to share with you significant spiritual experiences I've had that taught me how I now choose to make life easier on my path toward wholeness. These experiences are true and they did happen to me.

I thought I could handle the pain in my life by taking an "only the facts" approach, but that hasn't worked. I still try on occasion, but much less frequently now. My logical bent serves me well, professionally, however. I am proud of my accomplishments, and in my professional world, I need to think and act systematically in order to get the job done. The process of receiving my AA in Communications, BA in Public Administration, MA in Counseling, Ph.D. in Clinical Psychology, and working as a Superior Court mediator and consultant has cemented this thinking style.

I have a long resume, and I'd like to share some of it with you, not to trumpet my accomplishments, but to show you that the unlikely events in the story ahead have happened to someone who is very much a part of the mainstream. I also needed those accomplishments so others would accept me, and most of all, so I would accept myself. I dedicated many years to helping child victims and I am proud of that accomplishment. The children benefitted from my work, but so have I. I have come to realize that my drive to achieve was also a burning desire for approval from those with power. My goal was to help children, but it also had to do with feelings of self-worth about myself. For many years, I defined myself by my accomplishments. Now I know who I am without the labels.

For instance I spearheaded landmark legislation that established the foundation for a statewide computer system for missing, abused and exploited children. I also worked with the district attorney's office to initiate and coordinate a federal grant for county agencies working with child victims.

I served on two Attorney Generals' advisory boards that assisted law enforcement officials in tracking violent offenders and missing children. I co-authored the child safety curriculum standards for public schools in the nation, and have served as a special assistant to a United States Senator and as a consultant to a Governor. As a volunteer in a presidential campaign, I brought together mental health experts from throughout the country who created the children's agenda. That agenda was placed in a national political party platform. I have been the private guest of another President in the Oval Office of the White House.

For the past seven years, I have worked as a superior court child custody mediator, a research project consultant for child custody issues, and a forensic evaluator who testifies in court on child victim issues. I also serve on peer review panels for federal grant proposals.

As much as I value my analytical strengths and methods, they can get in the way of living from my heart, and may also limit my frame of reference. I have also come to realize that when I analyze, I am separating. I am separating thought from thought and concept from concept. My way of being in the world is now through connection, so analyzing and dissecting doesn't always fit with my spiritual philosophy. Having the ability to notice is the ultimate achievement. Awareness is all I need.

Even though my feet are firmly planted in this world, I feel privileged to see a world beyond it. Beneath the veil of consensual reality, compassionate love reigns and directs the course of my life through the law of synchronicity and free will.

In this world, I fulfill many roles: I am an adult woman, a friend, a daughter, a child and family therapist, a mother, a grandmother, and a victim-no-longer. I am a thinking and feeling person, and most importantly, a spiritual being. I have experienced many miracles in the moment. Biblical times do not have a monopoly on miracles or spiritual encounters. There is a voice inside that guides me, and the Light is my companion. Angels comfort me, protect me, and make their appearance known when they choose to do so, as they did by appearing in a photograph I took with a disposable paper camera while climbing the Himalayas.[1]

I have learned that in aligning myself to the greater will, alternately called unconditional love, the universe, the higher self, Prophet Mohammed, Jesus, Tao, Abraham, the Buddha or any words that resonate, I have discovered my true strength. My roots are in Christianity and I value those roots. I also value all thoughts, beliefs and feelings that allow total connection.

The concept of universal connection is not new. What is new is the accelerated rate at which universal connections are now being made. Mohandas Gandhi said,

"I believe in the essential unity of all that lives. Therefore I believe that if one person gains spiritually, the whole world gains, and if one person falls, the whole world falls to that extent."

Because of the connectedness between all things, there is meaning in every moment. Every moment is intricately synchronized far beyond imagination. Connection is my destiny, and along the way, I have struggled with issues of separation. I have learned that life's lessons are about separation; getting fired from a job, children leaving home, moving from one home to another, divorce and death. The infant is born, a cry is heard and separation has occurred. Separation is the hardest lesson in life. I can handle it much more easily now because I have come to realize that the only thing I "own" is my soul. I don't own anyone and I don't own material things. That doesn't mean I don't have material items such as a home and furniture; it just means I don't own them. A person can leave me voluntarily or involuntarily and a fire can rip away a home and furnishings in a flash of a second. When I become too attached, the lesson can be harder and swifter than I bargained for.

The experiences I am going to share with you have expanded my perception of the world. I can no longer look only to logic to guide me. Logic is the beginning of wisdom and not its center.

My frame of reference was first expanded with a most profound experience in my life. I was 22 years old at the time. The year was 1966.

On a Saturday in February, I left my three-year-old daughter, Kathy with my mother while I recuperated from a bad cold. I decided to spend the weekend in bed, treat myself with aspirin and orange juice, and take Monday off from work. On Wednesday, the day after Washington's birthday, I planned to return to work. *Stoic me.* I had no idea how ill I really was.

That Tuesday, February 22, is a day that has lived in my heart for almost twenty-nine years. I telephoned my mother early and asked her to look in on me if she was in the area. The chances of this were remote; we lived 45 minutes apart. This was the only way I could ask for help. For as long as I can remember and certainly since childhood, I have found it hard to express vulnerability or admit weakness.

Hearing my unusual request, my mother was able to interpret my distress signal. She decided to call my brother-in-law, a police officer in my hometown. He and his partner found me, called an ambulance, and got me to a hospital. I have no idea how much time elapsed between my call to my mother and my brother-in-law's arrival.

After I got off the phone with my mother, I laid on the maple twin bed in my bedroom. At some point, I saw a warm, alive, *compassionate* Light flood into the room from a corner in the ceiling. I wanted to be in that Light. I immediately lifted toward it and felt the deep desire to connect, to return home and become a part of the whole.

The essence of that Light is etched forever in my mind. I have never seen a Light with such brilliance. Its energy was not only compassionate, but conscious beyond all human comprehension.

When I looked back, I saw my body on the bed, an empty container that housed my soul. I felt no emotional attachment; it was nothing more than a discarded wrapper. I saw everything in the room simultaneously, and experienced a greater awareness of the connection between all things than I ever knew was possible. I saw a hairpin on the floor, a speck on the wall, a scratch on the dresser, all in the same instant. There was no need for space or accounting of time. There was only Oneness.

As I moved toward the Light, a gentle barrier emerged from it. The words, "learn and love" came into my awareness. I knew intuitively that I had not learned everything I was here to learn or loved everyone I was here to love.

I do not remember anything else. When I awakened, I was under an oxygen tent. The doctor told me my lungs had collapsed. The diagnosis was pneumonia, the flu and asthma.

I told my mother about the Light when she came to my bedside. She told me not to tell anyone because they probably wouldn't understand. For years, I never discussed it. My mother and I didn't understand it ourselves — there was nothing within our frame of reference that would explain such an occurrence.

It wasn't until ten years later, while having lunch with a good friend, that it felt safe enough for me to share my experience. She suggested I read Raymond Moody's **Life after Life**, a book about people who have had similar experiences. The book validated my experience. Thirty years later, I learned that the Buddhist religion believes in the White Light too. Everything is connected. This experience convinced me there was something more to life than what I had formerly believed. The Light permeates and surrounds me in every moment, and it gives me a sense of protection and balance. The Light is my companion.

My life after life experience was the first of three times I came close to death. The second time was the bus accident in 1990 and the third was during my trek in the Himalayas.

Mystical experiences do not only happen as the result of near death experiences. Connecting with the White Light is an ultimate mystical experience. I have been blessed to have the Light surround me throughout my life, and especially when I was in a great deal of pain. All these moments have brought me closer to my personal truth and my authentic self. They also bring me closer to others.

When my grandson Danny, who is Hispanic, Caucasian and Native American Indian, was three-years-old, he once said to me "we flew in the Light, G.G. We saw big *fish*. We saw flowers but we didn't smell the flowers." He wanted to know if we could smell the flowers the next time we flew in the Light. As I sat in awe listening to his tale, I told him that we could. Two years later, I asked him if he remembered telling me about our flying in the Light. His eyes flashed with recognition of that memory, he smiled and said he remembered. A few months later he asked me, "when we were flying in the Light, G.G. were we in an airplane?" Uh oh, his logical process was beginning to emerge. I respond, "Well, Danny we have *never* flown in a plane together." He thought for a moment, shrugged his shoulders and said, "well, we must have just flown in the Light." I nod and smile and find myself agreeing with him. We must have flown in the Light.

Six months after our last conversation, Danny was staying the week-end with me. He had a poster he wanted to hang up in my home. "Sure", I said, "Danny, where would you like to hang it up?" He used my scotch tape and very carefully placed the poster on the wall in my favorite room of the house. It took me several days to realize the significance of the poster. As I sat at my computer carefully crafting the last paragraph of this book, the connection was made. The poster has a large *whale* jumping out of the water. It sure looks like a big *fish* to me. I bet it does to Danny too.

I don't know where he gets what he knows but I do know society has not shut him down yet. Isn't that wonderful for him and for society! We have so much we can learn from the children.

My commitment to children is central in my personal and professional life. My need to build my self-esteem was not at the expense of children; it was in concert with helping children. I hope this book will give those of you who are parents a perspective that allows you to validate your childrens' spiritual knowledge and experiences. Perhaps it will also give you permission to listen to their wisdom. Children are our teachers. Don't be afraid if your child talks about things that you may not understand. Many of us don't "get it," when a child talks to us like Danny has done with me. What is being said just may not be within our frame of reference. Perhaps what the children are telling us is the most real of all.

I am also writing this so that you may learn from my struggles, and be open to experiencing new solutions. In this book I share the lessons I have learned about impermanence, the power of intention, compassion toward myself and others, the law of synchronicity, and the need to accept separation with dignity. Through these lessons, I have learned how to move toward connection within myself, the community and the world, and into greater wholeness.

I left for Nepal telling my family and friends that I felt I had "done it all". There didn't seem to be anything left for me to see or do. I had reached my professional peak and felt I had made a positive difference in many lives. Spiritually I had been given more than most. But while climbing up and coming down from the mountain, I came to realize I had not seen or done it all. Now I know that experiencing and living my wholeness is just beginning.

If I had consciously known, when I was a child, what I learned while in the Himalayas, my life might have taken a different path - one of ease and gentleness. Perhaps the telling of my struggles and successes will support you through your own life's experiences on a path toward wholeness. I wish that for each of you.

---

[1]The Angel picture was taken on the Wednesday before Christmas as I climbed toward Mt. Everest, the Tengboche monastery and His Holiness the Lama. The sherpa who was with me and I did not see anything unusual, such as a flare or cloud in the picture at the time it was taken. With free will, if you look very closely at the picture on the front cover of this book, you may see the angel who was on the path with us. The Circle of Rainbow Light was taken on Christmas Eve Day and is on the back cover of the book.

 CHAPTER ONE: **TAKE OFF!**

"You only have four minutes to catch your flight!", the Delta airlines representative looks at me with fear in her eyes and a strong sound of urgency in her voice.

"No, I have thirty minutes!" I look at the ticket. I am wrong. I had not double-checked the time.

She grabs my duffle bag and swings it onto the baggage conveyor belt, while both of us are hoping it will reach my plane as fast as I have to. Little do I know that the easiest part of my trip has just begun.

I grab my passport, traveler's checks and airline ticket as I try to push back the water bag on my shoulder to reach for my overnight bag. My 25-pound backpack is resting on my shoulders as I run as fast as I can toward the gate.

Oh no, I think. Look at the line at the security gate! I'll never make it to the plane!

The lady who is last in line suggests I run ahead; she assures me the others won't mind. She's right. They smile as they all wave me on. They understand that my plane is leaving in seconds and I have a long way to run.

They are definitely angels who are passing through my life. Or should I say I am passing through their lives? My definition of an angel is a benevolent being of Light. At this moment, I need all the angels I can get, and they have appeared as travelers. Their benevolent Light is sending me off on my chosen adventure.

So far, so good. But then a shrill, female voice stops me in my tracks. "Put that purse on the belt!"

Of course, I must put my overnight bag on the security conveyor belt. I retrace my steps and throw the bag on the moving belt and I, once again, run through the security arch.

The stern female voice yells again, "Come back and put your backpack on the belt!"

I forgot about my backpack! With frustration, I yank the buckles open and throw the backpack on the belt. It is moving faster through the monitor than I am through the gate. This should be it.

She yells again. "Take that black fannypack off your waist and put it on the belt!" This woman is bound and determined to make me jump through every hoop.

"Oh come on," I say. "There are no alarms going off. There is nothing in my waist purse except for papers!"

She looks at me sternly and doesn't give an inch. Her hands are on her hips. No time to argue.

I don't want to be in this struggle. With that, I fight with the difficult snap on my fannypack and throw it on the belt with a vengeance. I can practically see the airplane gaining speed as it heads down the runway. My anxiety is overwhelming. Now I can run!

She yells again and asks, "What is that on your shoulder?"

I turn and helplessly shrug my shoulders. "It's just a water bag. Just a simple little water bag filled with water; nothing more." She appears to be getting some perverse pleasure out of all this.

"Well, I don't know what's in it. I have to check it," she says, with a smirk surfacing on her face. Another power struggle, I think. Why do I have to keep learning this lesson?

"Well, it *is* water," I assert. "See for yourself." I open the cap and pour the water all over her assistant's hand and the belt. The assistant lets out a loud squeal. The people in line are gasping and laughing. If the security woman had been closer, I would have relished pouring it on *her* hand, but I've made my point. I grab my backpack, waist-strapped purse and water bag, and continue my race to the gate.

"You are so rude!," the security woman yells after me.

"The same to you," I yell back, with little more than a glance. Immediately I feel guilty for the harsh, separating words and my behavior, but I'm feeling more frustrated and afraid than guilty. I'm aware enough to know that my fear has created a barrier. I pride myself in thinking I am a spiritual being, but sometimes I disappoint me.

Delta Airlines Flight #1409 hasn't given up on me. The plane is waiting when I arrive. As I board, I notice a look of relief cross the flight attendant's face. No one is more relieved than I am in the moment. She helps me store my items in the overhead compartment and I find my seat.

The plane immediately takes off for Portland, Oregon. I am the passenger they were waiting for. I guess I am supposed to be on this plane. From Portland I will go on to Seoul, Korea; Taipei, Taiwan; Bangkok, Thailand; and ultimately, Kathmandu, Nepal and the Himalayas.

I am on my way.

For the last three years, I've given myself the gift of adventure for Christmas. This year, I am going on a three-week trek in the Himalayas where I am going to meet the Lama in a monastery at the highest of highs, near Mount Everest, on Christmas Day. Nothing is more important to me than meeting the Lama, and I am a Christian! I don't even know what a Buddhist Lama does, but I can't wait to arrive at the Monastery and meet him. Nothing could have kept me from this - not a security guard, not my friends' concerns, not even my doctor's warnings.

I sit quietly, close my eyes and catch my breath. Then I take a deep breath, the first one I have had in ten minutes. All of a sudden it hits me - *where is my overnight bag with my New Year's dress in it?* I experience a moment of panic and mention it to the passenger sitting next to me.

"As long as you have your passport and traveler's checks, don't worry about it," he reassures me. "You can always buy a new dress in Bangkok."

I start to laugh, and pat my waist purse, certain I have my passport and traveler's checks. There's nothing to worry about. I close my eyes and lean further into the soft First Class seat; my free frequent flyer miles upgrade came in handy since I would rather be sitting here than in the economy section. I shake my head as I think back at what happened at the security checkpoint. I know better than to behave the way I had in the airport, and I must remember the Golden Rule and treat people the way I want to be treated. Good theory, hard to practice. I even struggled with my doctor about going on this trip.

A few weeks earlier, she told me in no uncertain terms, "I do not want you to go. I have a very bad feeling about you taking this trip." There was no medical reason for her concern; it was purely her intuition.

I, too, had fears about taking this trip, but I decided not to let those fears deter my plans. Weeks ago, I wrote in my journal: *Now I am going to Nepal and to Mt. Everest, the highest of highs on Christmas Day with the Lama, and for the past two weeks, every time I think about the trip the thought overwhelms me, "I won't be coming back."*

I've told this to my friends and they repeatedly urged me not to go. I told my doctor what I wrote in my journal and it puzzled her.

"What do you mean by that?" she asked me during our visit.

"I don't know. I only know what I have written in my journal" That thought felt real. I didn't have a death wish. Perhaps I meant the old Jerri Curry wouldn't be coming back. I just know I have to be there.

"Well, you have two weeks to convince me," she had said. Come back and prove you've been working out regularly and that you are fit to take this trip. I will do everything in my power to keep you from going if you can't reassure me that you should go."

I told her I had been walking two or three hours every day, using my treadmill and climbing some local hills to get in shape. I promised I would be ready for the trip. I just wanted to live my life fully and completely. No shades of gray, but in full technicolor. I like rainbows.

I broke the tension by telling her what I had come to realize, "I am not sure why I am going. I don't even know what Lamas do." We laughed. I then asked her for something to help me ward off the infrequent but severe headaches I sometimes get. She gave me some altitude sickness medicine called Acetazolamide. The medicine would keep me from getting a bad headache and nausea (both symptoms of altitude sickness), as long as I started taking it in Bangkok, she said.

Despite my doctor's feelings of foreboding, and my own fears, deep down I knew I had to make this trip. I thought I would be fine. One good sign was the double rainbow that appeared in the sky the day before my departure. When I was getting my hair cut, my beautician called my attention to a double rainbow outside the window. To my utter delight, I saw a second one as I drove home later that day — crowning the roof of my home. This one seemed to stay in place for the longest time, and it seemed as though it was resting on my doorstep as I entered my home. Double rainbows are special.

Double rainbows don't happen very often, I am told. I took it as a sign that this trip was spiritual and it was important. A double rainbow, like an angel, is a great symbol. I smiled quietly to myself when I saw them.

I also know I am on the right path when doors open easily. Months earlier, I had initially signed up for the "Everest Escapade" rather than the "Everest Adventure," which is what I am on now. The Escapade itinerary would have had us at the Tengboche Monastery on Christmas Day. The Adventure would have us there a couple of days earlier and we would be going back down the mountain on Christmas Day. I wanted to meet the Lama at the monastery with Mt. Everest nearby on Christmas Day. To be at the highest of highs on my holy holiday was important to me. I asked the travel agent the difference between the two tours and he said the Escapade would mean sleeping in tents while the Adventure would have us staying in lodges. I thought I was sturdy enough for a tent, but then he said we would get a bowl of hot water in the lodges and drinking water only if we were in the tents. I asked how large the bowl was and he said, it was not very large, but it was larger than a cup. Well, the decision was made. I traded Christmas Day at the monastery with the Lama for a hot bowl of water. I wasn't happy, but now I knew I could be bought. The price was a bowl of hot water to care for my basic hygiene needs for several weeks. I let it go and accepted my disappointment about not being at the monastery on Christmas Day. I kept the disappointment to myself.

Two months later, the final itinerary was mailed out. The Adventure itinerary had changed. We would be staying at the Tengboche Monastery on Christmas Eve and Day! And, we would be getting a bowl of hot water and sleeping in beds, too. Isn't synchronicity great? And I had not complained to anyone. Perhaps the angels thought I

23

deserved both a bowl of hot water *and* the Lama on Christmas Day. I will be at the highest of highs on the Christian holy day.[1]

The other thing that lessened my fears about this trip was my self-confidence. I have prided myself on being a lady who knows how to take care of herself. I am independent, accomplished and strong. I've had to be. After my first divorce, at age 19, I supported myself and my infant child by working as a salesperson in a record store, helping other teenagers buy their favorite records. I also had to leave my daughter with a baby sitter during that time, and it was difficult for both of us.

As a single teen mother, I took care of my daughter and myself. Later, I worked as a file clerk for a bank, and then I became a teller. I went to legal secretarial school, even though that meant leaving my daughter with a baby sitter for many nights while I drove the two hour trip between my home and the school. My career climb was not easy.

In 1972, I became involved in politics. My involvement brought me into the world of illusion, as played out in the national political arena, and I was successful almost every step of the way. I was ambitious and hard working. This allowed me to get things done. It also provided me with the image I was seeking. A "together" woman who could take care of herself.

I had worked on a presidential campaign for a United States Senator, and for the Democratic National Committee. Working for the chairman of that committee, Robert Strauss, was a privilege. He eventually became an ambassador to President Bush. Several years later, I worked for the Bush administration as a consultant on child abuse issues.

When I look back, I realize that Mr. Strauss and his staff were angels in my political life, as were President and Mrs. Jimmy Carter. As their personal friend, I was their private guest in the Oval Office of the White House many years ago. The

President's integrity was obvious to me, and he always treated me with professional respect and warmth. I consider both of them to be earth angels.

After working for a national political party and later a United States Senator, I decided to associate with a popular governor. That decision became extremely painful because, during that time two senior aides — independent of each other — began to sexually harass me. One harassment led to a sexual assault and the other to a rape. It was rape because I was not a willing participant. That was long before sexual harassment was recognized by law as immoral and criminal. Although I discussed the specifics with my boyfriend, my minister, members of the women's movement and a reporter who promised confidentiality until I gave him permission to publish my story, I chose not to make the accusations public.

My minister said people who behave that way would have nothing to fear if they, at anytime, apologized to the victim and expressed regret in their actions; then public exposure would probably not occur. Neither man ever apologized to me, and I went through many years of pain because of these incidents. It cost me a great deal emotionally. I responded by closing off and not trusting men. To protect myself from becoming injured in that way again, I became much more aggressive in the business world. My ability to express my vulnerability and my openness for support by men almost disappeared. One could say I learned too well. The balance between my masculine and feminine energy was tipped in the masculine's favor so that I could survive in the working world. Perhaps many working women have experienced similar feelings.

By the time of this trip, I need balance, and I wonder in these quiet moments of reflection on the plane, if my trip to the Himalayas will teach me to share without giving away pieces of myself. It is called keeping the integrity of my soul.

As Betty J. Eadie said in her book, **Embraced By The Light:**

> *"Each experience was a tool for me to grow by. Every unhappy experience*
> *had allowed me to obtain greater understanding of myself until I learned to*
> *avoid those experiences.... Sometimes, I had many guardian angels around*
> *me, sometimes, just a few, depending upon my needs."*

The pain of being in the world of politics was wrenching. But through politics, I was able to meet people who had integrity and who were dedicated to trying to make this a better world, especially for children, and I joined in those worthy ventures.

For example, I spearheaded efforts that led to the passage of landmark legislation to help law enforcement officials track missing and exploited children. John Brodie, an employee of the California Department of Justice, was instrumental in making this legislation a reality. His willingness to speak up for what was needed nearly cost him his career. Government employees with heart do continue to exist in our system; I worked with many for the good of children.

Ten-year-old Kevin Collins, who was abducted by a stranger while walking home from school in San Francisco, was one of the angels who inspired me in that effort. My desire to help find him and keep other children from being kidnapped became the priority in my life. As a mother, I could not think of anything worse than not knowing where my daughter was or what she might be going through. This is one of the most painful separations anyone has to face. I know well from my own experience and from my work as a child custody mediator, how hard such separation can be.

I became a child custody superior court mediator and child custody and forensic evaluator in an effort to bring people together at one of the most difficult separation experiences in life - divorce. Learning to handle separation with grace and dignity is the most difficult challenge in life. As a mediator, I have a priority in bringing people together, if not as a couple, then in positive roles as parents for their children.

In 1988, I led a National Children's Agenda with twenty experts throughout the country for a national political platform. In addition, I coordinated, with the district attorney's office in my county, bringing a federal grant to our agencies to help missing and exploited children. My reward was knowing child victims would be helped, as well as the fact that I gained an image that was endorsed by the powers of society. I, myself, was accepted as "an expert," and given the credibility I craved so I could feel good about myself as a person and not see myself as a victim.

One of the proudest moments of my professional life was when the federal government sent me to Decatur, Illinois, to help the community set up a multi-disciplinary program so their agencies could work together to help child victims. At the end of the training, I stood up and told those dedicated people that working with them had been a heartfelt experience for me. As I left for the airport, the participants gave me a standing ovation. One woman came out into the aisle and hugged me. It was the first time anyone had ever gotten a standing ovation in M/CAP (Missing And Exploited Children Comprehensive Action Program), and it took my breath away to have that type of acknowledgement from my peers.

My eyes watered as I rode in the taxi to the small airport in Decatur. As I boarded my plane, I glanced back and saw a group of little boys standing in the terminal, waving excitedly, their faces pressed to the window. From my seat, I could still see them waving. I felt they might be saying "Thank you, Dr. Jerri, for coming to Decatur to help us." I could not prevent the tears from rolling down my cheeks as I waved back. I felt connected to those children and to my cause. These professional experiences are shared to emphasize the significance I have placed on children and victims throughout my life. In many ways, it is my life. No longer needing the label itself, it is, in part, who I am. I value children as well as positive contributions to our community. The healing for all of us helps make the world a better place.

The Decatur trip was a peak experience. I've known valleys, as well. I was married three times. What I will say about those relationships is: one marriage taught me about abuse; another taught me how painful it is when I try to please another at my own expense, and thereby give away pieces of myself; and the other one taught me more than I ever wanted to know about betrayal.

Amazing how one paragraph can describe a lifetime of both pain and pleasure in significant relationships. It may be because my heart has now healed from those experiences. We know we have healed when the emotional charge connected to the negative experience has been released.

Now I know those marriages were not failures. They offered very important lessons and taught me about yet another form of separation. It has been my goal, in my personal and professional life, to overcome separation. I teach what I need to learn.

In the process, I have had to learn to honor each change with grace. Believe me, when change first hits, I go kicking and screaming through it. Often, I receive guidance from a source beyond myself.

For instance, somehow I knew, in the course of my third marriage, that it was important to begin to prepare for my financial independence. I signed up for college, and after twelve years, received a Ph.D. in clinical psychology and obtained my license as a marriage and family child therapist. I couldn't have known then that my third marriage would end, but my inner voice kept urging me on in my education and out of that relationship. I honored my integrity by following that inner voice. It was my best life decision, even though it was hard to believe at the time.

My divorces were valuable lessons for me. Through each lesson in life, I have learned to become the person I now am, and I wouldn't trade any part of myself for the world.

Some of those lessons were with me when I nearly lost my daughter. On May 11, 1979, St. Rose Hospital in Hayward, California telephoned me. The phone was ringing as I walked in the front door. "Yes, I have a sixteen-year-old daughter named Kathleen. You want me to come to the hospital right away?"

There had been an automobile accident.

I was pulling out of the garage when my husband drove up and he jumps into the car with me. As we raced through the front doors of the hospital, two doctors walked toward us. I remember thinking, please, God, not *two* doctors. If it takes two, the news must be very bad.

My daughter, Kathy, whom I had raised alone for the first fifteen years of her life, was not expected to live. She had severe head injuries and was in a coma. Yes, I could see her for a moment, but they had to treat her immediately. We were escorted to a private holding room where she was lying on a steel slab. Lines of dried blood ran from her ears onto her cheeks. She wasn't moving. My legs buckled and the doctors caught me as I began to fall. I think they let me touch her for a moment. Then I had to leave, but I didn't want to leave her. I walked toward the door, looking back, and prayed I would see her again. We had to be together. I remember praying silently, please God, let me see her again. Separation is so hard! Nothing is harder. Nothing.

Despite my fear, I kept hoping she would be fine. I called a friend, Myrl, and told her "...find George. There had been a terrible accident." My minister, George, showed up at the hospital a short time later. He told me the church would do a healing service for Kathy on Sunday. That was at a time when I had no idea what a healing service was. Even though I had had several spiritual experiences in the past, the concept of an *actual healing experience* didn't fit into my frame of reference.

Days had passed. I was in a fog. My daughter was in a coma and not expected to live. No one expected her to live; no one that is, but me. I was sure Kathy would recover, even though the doctors had expressed very little hope. Was this denial or a sense of certainty? The inner voice assured me she would be with us for a very long time. On a Sunday morning, my husband and I were eating breakfast at a nearby restaurant when a soft silent voice, a voice impression really, urged me to return to the hospital immediately. We had no time to finish eating. We had to go!

As we raced into her intensive care room, which was connected with a window to the nurse's station, I could see that the room was lit up with a bright white Light.

The nurse was bending over Kathy and talking to her: "What is your name? Do you know where you are? Come on sweetie, talk to me," the nurse said.

She turned to us and said, "Your daughter is coming up very fast. Really fast. I can't explain why or how she is coming up this fast."

Kathy told the nurse her name was Klinker. That name eventually had a special place in my heart. Years later, I used the name Klinker, the Rainbow Clown, in a family fairy tale I had written.[2]

George called an hour later. He told me the church completed a healing service for Kathy at the same time I entered her room, and saw the Light. Later, a church friend described the church as "lit up with a big bright white Light," while the service was held.

As my friend, Tom, later explained it to me, George had put on some music and asked the congregation to close their eyes, and be with Kathy in whatever way she wanted to be with them. He asked that they not try to force her to live. That had to be Kathy's decision. Tom said he saw himself standing with Kathy on top of the Golden Gate Bridge. He was trying to convince her to fly around the bay with him, but she wouldn't do it. He took off like Peter Pan, flew around Mt. Tamalpais, and scooped down over Angel Island. Another angel in my life.

Tom said he went back to the top of the bridge and put his hand out so Kathy could fly with him. He knew she would be fine, he said, when she took his hand and they flew off together.

While Kathy was in the coma, a former boyfriend, with whom she had problems in the past, broke into her room and tried to wake her while she was on life support. We considered a restraining order, but the nurse assured us he would not get in her room again.

Later, when Kathy came out of the coma, it was clear to me she had regressed. When we walked through the hospital corridor, my 16-year-old daughter would hold my hand and swing it like a little girl about the age of seven. She asked me to put her hair in braids with pink ribbons. She said she liked pink ribbons "a lot." Luckily, she wouldn't need *physical* rehabilitation, but I didn't know if she would ever be the same again.

Eventually the doctors allowed her to come home. She acted younger and much more vulnerable, but overall she seemed to function at her pre-accident level. Sometime after coming home, she told me she and her former boyfriend — the one who had broken into her hospital room — were getting back together. I just looked at her and I felt confused. She had come so far in her recovery. Why would she want to be with a boyfriend who had caused her so many problems prior to the accident? *Has she survived,* I wondered, *just so she can experience more hurt in her life?* Not knowing what to say, I walked into my bedroom and stood at the dresser, when a charge card receipt of my husband's caught my eye. I knew instantly my husband had not been where he'd said he was several days earlier. I didn't understand, but I knew it would be too painful to ask why. I walked to the living room and picked up my purse and car keys. I didn't have on my shoes, but it didn't seem to matter very much. At that moment, I just did not want to know or be part of the choices my daughter and my husband seemed to be making in their lives.

It was July 15, 1979 - another significant day in my life.

In my bare feet, I began driving north. When I realized I wasn't wearing shoes, I stopped and purchased a cheap pair of sandals. Late that night I stopped at a motel. I thought I might drive to Eureka and visit a friend. A few hours earlier, I called my family and told them I needed time alone to sort things out. I said I would be back, but I didn't know when.

That night in the motel room I knelt by the bed and prayed for guidance. The next morning I continued driving north. Around 10 a.m., I came to a rest stop and, for some reason, I decided to stop the car and walk around. I saw a huge redwood tree, sat on the bench beneath it and began to pray. I asked God to take over. I wanted to *let go and let God*. I was tired of trying to control everything and everyone, particularly myself. I just wanted rest.

As I sat there, the words, *"Thou shall not criticize"* came to me. That seemed appropriate because, many times, I had judged others harshly and unfairly. The highway was at my back and the harshness of the loud trucks and the heat from the asphalt helped me feel deeply what that meant. I returned to my car and continued driving.

Eventually I came to a lodge called the Hartsook Inn, nestled in the heart of the Redwoods. Behind the cabins was a trail that led me to the top of the knoll. There I found two redwood trees in a "V" shape reaching toward the sky. At the base of the trees were ferns that seemed to serve as an altar. I looked up and saw the sun shining down through the trees so that the rays of morning sun rested at my feet. I knelt, because it was the right thing to do. I was in the house of God. I was silent.

The words, *"Thou shall be humble"* came to me. There had been little of that in my life. I knew, instead, there had been too much bragging about things I had accomplished and people I knew. I suddenly realized how unimportant those things were. Kneeling before those gigantic trees, I felt the meaning of humility.

I continued my drive, eventually arriving at the Eel River. I pulled off the road and walked toward it. I removed my shoes and placed my feet in the cool running water.

People were swimming further downstream and two small children were trying very hard to put their large rubber rafts at the top of the gentle rapids. The water was only ankle deep, but it must have seemed monumental to them. They managed to get their raft to float past me, and into the rapids. It was quite an accomplishment for the little ones.

As I watched the children, the words, *"Accomplish in my Name,"* reached my awareness. The words came from within. With that thought firmly placed in my heart and mind, I returned to my car and continued my drive.

A state park was on my left and it seemed important to pull in and walk around. I told the park ranger at the gate I would only be a few minutes, and she waved me through without charging admission. I followed the sign that said "river trail," walked through a grove of shady trees, and came to a sandy beach. The water was calm and peaceful. I stood by the water's edge and the words, *"Be calm within your heart,"* were spoken silently.

I was feeling very calm by then, because I realized my inner guidance was with me. I also knew in that moment that I was on a journey not necessarily of my own making. I had chosen to let God lead me on a path unknown. This had been my prayer since I'd left my home.

I was experiencing grace, but I didn't know it in the moment. I just knew it was something beyond my doing.

As I continued on, I came across a giant redwood tree that had fallen near the road. The roots had been pulled from the ground, still attached to the base of the tree. As I touched it, I felt the word 'strength.' Nothing else seemed to come through. I then walked down a narrow path leading alongside that tree, stopped suddenly, and looked up toward the sky. I was surrounded by a circle of redwood trees.

"Surround yourself with inner strength," was the fifth message. I knelt, and felt blessed that these messages were being given to me. I returned to the car, and further down the road, came upon the Eel River once again.

At the shore's edge, I removed my shoes and slipped my feet again into the gentle, cool water. Upstream I saw the majestic mountains off in the distance, and a few rolling clouds against an extraordinarily blue sky. Its color matched the water, and the effect was lovely. The words, *"Be gentle with your friends and love to your enemies,"* were given to me. I sat for some time taking in the words and the intention behind them.

As I drove further down the road, I came to the town of Fortuna. Fortuna is about 20 miles south of Eureka (my friend's home, and what I originally thought was my destination). The inner voice told me to pull off there and buy gasoline. Consciously, I doubted that a Texaco station would be open and that was the only credit card I had with me. I felt my chance of getting gas with my credit card would be better in Eureka, because of the gasoline crisis. The voice impression promised me that, even though it was Sunday, there would be a Texaco station open just for me. So I turned off, and the first station I came to was Texaco. I bought the gas from a young man who said his boss told him he didn't have to open today, but since he hadn't anything else to do, and there was a little gas left, he decided to open. I smiled, thanked him, and paid for the gas.

Then I pulled my car off to the side of the station to fill up the water tank. I was not sure why I should be so concerned with the water tank but it seemed important to check it at that time. As I was trying to get the cap off — with some difficulty — two young angels approached me. They asked if I needed help and I told them I did. They were kind enough to remove the cap and I filled up the tank with water. I left the town of Fortuna, feeling more secure that my car was in good shape for the journey.

At the next turnoff, I was told to go to Ferndale. I never did make it to Eureka, though I wasn't far away. I drove to the top of the ridge overlooking the town, stopped my car and got out. I looked down upon the valley of Ferndale with its green pastures, rolling green mountains and white church steeple. It was beautiful. I turned to the other side of the ridge and saw miles of redwood trees. Then I looked at my feet and saw the most perfect purple flower in full bloom; the words, *"Through awareness, bring beauty to the world"* came to me. Yes, I knew I could do that, and I continued the journey. I did not know what was next, but I was open to listening and learning. I felt very peaceful in the totality of that experience.

I drove toward the coast thinking it might be a perfect place to be inspired. Once I reached it, I walked to the edge of the road, and watched the waves crashing against the shore. I waited and waited. Nothing happened and no words were spoken. I realized then that I could not set up a moment of inspiration. It had to happen when God chose to speak and when I was open enough to listen and release the need to control. With that understanding, I returned to my car and drove toward the mountains. About an hour later, I came across an old, weather beaten barn that looked very much like it might topple with the next burst of wind. I walked toward the barn and reached out to the old tattered fence, erected to keep out intruders. I placed my hand on the fence, noticing that the gate attached to it was as new as the fence was old. As I ran my fingers across the old, decrepit fence and the shining gate, the words, *"Care for the old and cherish the new,"* came to me. I smiled, knowing God and the angels had touched me once again.

As I started into the mountains, I came to a fork in the road and instantly knew to take the road to the right. I drove a mile, then I left the paved road and began driving along a dusty, narrow path. As I climbed the mountain, I saw erosion from rain storms in the dirt road. The road was so steep, I couldn't see over the edge to the bottom of the valley. When I looked to my right, however, I noticed how the mountain climbed straight up.

I continued driving for three more hours, but saw no cars, people or other signs of civilization. Deer were feeding on the mountainside, and brooks of rushing water flowed down to the road. My car drove through the water, and sometimes my tires stuck for a moment in the crevices. Then, with some resistance, they continued on.

Often the back tires would skid and start to slide toward the mountain's edge. It dawned on me that if my car went over the side, it would be weeks, perhaps months, before anyone would find me. Fear overtook me, and I started to cry. I asked God what was wanted of me and I heard "Continue." Finally the Voice said, "Stop at the next stream and wash your face and drink from the water." I drove through the next water crossing, stopped my car and set the brake — not to do so would cause the car to slide down the mountainside. I walked toward the running water, knelt, washed my face and drank the clear, cool water. I received another message, but its full meaning did not come to me until later. The message was: *"Through faith all fears are conquered."*

I returned to my car, and continued driving. About a half hour later, and with desperation and an overwhelming sense of panic in my heart, I asked the Voice once again what it wanted from me. It was becoming dark, the sun was going down very quickly, and I didn't know what was ahead. I just knew I could not travel on this road after dark.

Should I try to back down the road for three plus hours? Of course not! That would not make any sense. Should I stop and sleep and wait for daybreak? Please, tell me, what should I do? The Voice only said, "Continue." I cried, but I heeded the message.

My eyes blurred by tears, I could hardly see the road ahead of me. As my car inched up the narrow mountain trail, I thought of the fears that had overwhelmed me from the past. There was so much fear. I continued to cry. Slowly and reluctantly my car pulled around the curve, and then I saw the main paved road with cars going by in both directions! I stopped the car and sobbed even harder, but this time it was tears of relief; the message truly touched me.

The fears of the past three and one-half hours had kept me from enjoying the scenery of the mountains and streams. The quietness and beauty surrounding me had almost gone unnoticed. I had missed much in my life because of fear: fear of rejection, fear of jealousy, fear of failure, and so many other fears I had refused to face and release. What a waste it had been. I knew, then, the message would have significant meaning for me. With faith, I would no longer feel fear about what might or might not happen in my life.

By that time, it had become pitch black. As I drove down the paved road, I heard the rushing water from the river nearby. I stopped the car, walked across the road, and stood and listened to the river. I felt the words, but thought, "there is no sign and therefore I am not sure of the message." With that, I returned to my car and drove on. Looking back I realize I still had not gotten it! I thought I had to have a sign instead of simply depending on my inner knowing.

A short time later, while driving out of the mountains, the Voice said, "Turn off on this side road." I did, but not without protest. "Please God, I am not up to another dusty road. Please don't send me in that direction." But with faith, I did turn off, and within 20 feet of the highway, I came to a locked gate. I could go no further. As I started to turn my car around, I looked out of the car window and saw a most unusual sight. Against the black night stood a giant white tree with branches reaching toward the stars. The starkness of its whiteness was highlighted by the black night backdrop. It was a beautiful and stunning sight, this incredible white tree, with its thousand of branches connecting and reaching out. Again the words came, *"Bring forth my Word, through Me you are One."*

With that newfound knowledge, I started for home. It had been a day of growth, a day of joy, a day of intense feeling and peace. I was tired and knew I needed to rest. I stopped at a motel and slept peacefully. Upon rising, I knew I was going home.

When I arrived, I decided to take a shower and freshen up. As I was in the shower I held my head under the cool running water and I felt a glow of incredible Light streaming over and through me. At that moment I realized I had been gone for forty hours. After the shower, I got a map out of the drawer and looked for the location where I had been the day before. I found it. The name was "King's Peak."

As the days wore on, my ego began to tell me the experience did not happen. It was all my imagination. This inner struggle continued as I drove downtown to run some errands. I wondered if it had really happened. As I sat at a corner waiting for the light to turn green, I looked to my right and saw a new apartment complex being built. The entrance sign read "The Redwoods."

Everything speaks to me. I've come to realize that, although signs are given to help us, they are really not necessary when we learn to trust our inner voice and inspiration. It is then we can live by the grace of God.

Some time later, I was having lunch with my friend, Father John LoSchiavo, chancellor of the University of San Francisco, and I shared the experience with him.

"Jerri, what are you going to do with this?"

"I don't know," I told him. "I guess, just keep it to myself and enjoy it, and find comfort in the words."

For 15 years, I let it go at that. From time to time I would wonder, how was I to use this loving guidance?

Little do I know, as the plane carries me to Portland, the first leg of my journey to the Himalayas, that I am about to undergo the ordeal that will allow me to fully live from this wisdom and to eventually share it with you. So many memories. So many moments - some magic and some tragic and life goes on.

---

[1]I learned much later His Holiness Rinpoche Ngawang Tenzing Jangpo of the Tengboche Monastery was the highest ranking Lama in Nepal.

[2]The nine family fairy tales are parables: 1) Klinker (special needs). Klinker, the Rainbow Clown runs away from the circus because he is different. He has a multi-striped face and the other clowns have solid color faces; 2) Shy Violet (self-esteem); 3) Puffer (friendships); 4) Snowflake (control); 5) David and the Musical Miracle Merry-Go-Round (positive attitude); 6) Old Ollie the Octopus (fear); 7) Star (identity); 8) Buttercup and the butterflies (competition); 9) and The Swan (commitment).

# CHAPTER TWO: **THE TREK THAT ALMOST WASN'T**

The captain's voice comes through the intercom, "We will be landing in Portland in a few minutes". I learn that it will be a short layover and then we will fly on to Seoul, through Taipei, and then overnight in Bangkok and then to my final destination, Nepal.

It has been an easy flight to Portland. I notice the presence of ease. That happens so seldom in my life. I am at rest with the memories that have flowed through my mind. Many thoughts. Many memories. A life of pain. A life of principle and one of pleasure some of the time.

Oh yes, the uneasy part. I better report my missing New Year's Eve bag to the Delta reservation clerk. Perhaps an agent in San Francisco can go to the security gate and pick up the bag and hold it until I return from Nepal in January. She is on the phone and I wait impatiently. I am not late for my plane to Bangkok; just ordinary impatience that is part of my normal routine. I tap the counter. I look at my watch. I raise my eyebrows in her direction. She seems not to notice. She is ignoring my impatience and there doesn't seem to be anything I can do. I wait with a frown on my face.

Now we can talk about my bag in San Francisco. Yes, she will have someone from Delta pick it up and hold it. Is there anything valuable in it? No, I shake my head with certainty. Nothing more than a white party skirt and sweater, a pair of evening high heels, nylons and a curling iron for my hair for New Year's Eve in Bangkok. I will buy a new dress after my trip to Nepal.

I easily pass through the gate to board my plane with a first stop in Seoul, Korea. The attendant takes my ticket and I find my seat in the business section. The big, soft seats make all the difference in an international flight. My backpack is stored safely in the overhead compartment. My water jug is laying near my feet on the floor and my waist purse is resting securely against my stomach. My money belt is under my sweater securely fastened. I have chosen two paperback books for this trip. One is entitled **Destiny** (Beauman, 1987) and the other, **Acts of Faith** (Erich Segal, 1992). They sound like intriguing titles for a trip to the Himalayas. The titles seem to connect with my trip but I don't know how in this moment and maybe I will never know how. That is all right too. I am not supposed to know how everything connects together. I am just supposed to be aware that everything does connect. That is all I need to know. Now I am fine and ready to have a wonderful experience. The adventure begins as I close my eyes and rest my head against the soft seat that is supporting my already weary body.

My thoughts return to earlier this morning. The alarm clock had gone off before daylight. Wearing the twenty-five pound backpack was a challenge. I stepped onto an airporter shuttle near my home earlier that morning. Rainbows were painted on the side of the bus. Rainbows appear again. I smiled silently.

Oh yes, I have rainbow and angel stickers in my backpack. The travel agent told me not to take candy for the village children. The children don't have the opportunity to visit a dentist and the sugar will hurt their teeth. I hope they like the stickers.

Two men smiled as I slowly stepped onto the rainbow-adorned bus. We began talking immediately. One was a teacher who was traveling north to visit with family members he had not connected with in a very long time. He was excited about the coming connection. The other was visiting from Bangkok. I raised my eyebrows in surprise. Interesting! I don't believe in coincidences anymore. I was aware of synchronicity during our conversation. The visitor from Bangkok gave me some ideas on things to see while I am there. The sights sound intriguing. Maybe I should stay an extra day in Bangkok *but no*, the plan is in place and it is beyond trying to change it now.

The teacher asked me where I was going. I told him about my plans to trek in the Himalayas. The questions came rapidly. "Was I a single woman traveling alone...did I speak Nepalese...how long would I be gone...had I ever trekked before...was I in good shape for that type of experience...how heavy was my backpack...who was going with me...did I have the right equipment...do I usually take such adventurous trips." Both men seem intrigued, but also somewhat concerned about this adventure. I reassured them I could take care of myself, little knowing the lessons that lay ahead. I had become comfortable doing things on my own, so I would be fine. No problem.

It was a pleasant drive to the airport. We arrived and I asked one of the men if he would take a picture of me by the rainbow painted bus. Afterwards we said our goodbyes and wished each other well. Then I learned I had four minutes to catch my plane. But that is behind me now.

The international flight crew appear to be helpful. Dinner is served and the movie will help pass the time. The flight over Alaska and the Bering Sea past Russia is uneventful. We cross the international dateline and lose a day as we head toward an ancient land. I have traveled at Christmas for the past several years because my only child and I have been separated. That means I have also been separated from my grandson who is the light of my life. It is too painful to think about, but sometimes think and feel I must.

Separation is the hardest lesson in life. I miss my daughter and grandson terribly, but pride and lack of skills prevents us from reconnecting. I know better than that, but the theory on the importance of connection is often hard to practice. How do we get to this place of pride and separation? I am still learning.

After dinner I close my eyes as the cabin becomes dark. We are headed for Seoul, Korea. The plane becomes very quiet. As I lean further into the seat, my hand rests on my waist-strapped purse. I pat it. I have my passport. I have my traveler's checks. Again, I pat my waist purse with reassurance. My eyes glance down at the purse. I *know* I have them. I put them in there as I ran toward the security gate. I know I did.

Well, I think I did. I unzip my waist strapped purse. There are some papers, but I don't see a blue passport. I don't see a blue wallet with traveler's checks. They must be in here! They have to be here. I stand up and search my pockets. I check my hidden money belt under my sweater. Where are they?

A flight attendant is walking past me. I stop him with a whimper. "You can't be serious. You have to have your passport! We are stopping in Korea and you will have to get off the plane with the rest of us. They won't let you back on the plane without your passport!" I have looked everywhere. I can't find my passport or my traveler's checks. I begin to cry. His concern comes through loud and clear. He lifts my backpack out of the overhead compartment. We carry all of my belongings to the crew quarters. I am sitting on the floor pulling everything out but there is no passport; there are no traveler's checks. They are not on this plane. They are probably still in San Francisco. I am not sure. Maybe I left them in Portland. I don't remember if the Delta representative asked for my passport there.

The flight attendant who had helped me tells the chief flight attendant and her mouth falls open. She begins to look at me suspiciously. It is the first of many suspicious looks I receive during the next two days. Losing a passport on any international flight is not good. We are thirty minutes outside of Seoul, Korea. No one headed for Korea can lose their passport! Several of the attendants help me go through my bags. I am embarrassed. How could I have lost my passport and traveler's checks? Aren't I an independent, self-sufficient, take charge woman? I will have to leave the plane with everyone else once we land in Seoul. It is a security regulation. There are no exceptions. None. As I am crying my feeling of helplessness becomes obvious and overwhelming. Separation is the hardest lesson in life. I must stay on the plane. The plane is American property. I am safe here. I am told no. I must get off with everyone else. What will the Koreans do to me?

"We don't know," the chief attendant tells me. "We will make sure the next chief attendant knows about you. Don't worry. Yes, the crew is leaving the flight in Seoul. It will be alright," as she puts her arm around me. I can't believe how much crying I have been doing and the trip is just starting. What is next?

I walk cautiously off the plane. I don't want to leave the security of the plane, but I have no choice. The crew leaves and one crew member remains waiting for the other crew members to show up.

Now the Korean airport officials know I am in their airport without a passport. They look me over very carefully. "Is she telling the truth?", is written all over their faces. One woman's face shows she is not going to believe anything I say, no matter what. Is this instant payback time? If karma exists, is the San Francisco security guard laughing at this very moment? The Korean airport official is not easily persuaded. She won't allow me to get on the plane and leave for Bangkok. Everything feels so hard.

They are telling me in difficult to understand English, "You must stay here in detention. You will not go any further!" I am crying. I don't think they understand anything I am saying except that I don't have a passport. The airline attendant stands by helplessly. The plane is going to take off without me. Where will they take me? How long will I be there? What will it take to get me out of here? I have some U.S. currency. I know I don't have my passport or traveler's checks. I don't even know who to call.

Two Delta airline pilots in uniform approach the counter. They have been sitting in the reception area waiting to board the plane as passengers. They introduce themselves to me. They are flying to Taipei and will be the pilots for the plane to Bangkok. I didn't catch all of that then. It registers later. They introduce themselves to the airport officials. They ask me what has happened and I tell them. I tell them I have business cards, my driver's license, my credit cards and $168 in U.S. currency in my money belt. Well, not all is lost. The pilots are sure I am who I say I am and they smile as they shake my hand.

They begin to talk to the Korean officials. I do not understand the entire conversation but the general idea comes through. One pilot says, no, Dr. Curry, is not going to stay in Seoul, Korea. She is coming with us. None of the passengers or crew are leaving without her. If she stays, you will have all of the other Americans staying, along with the Delta Airlines crew of the plane. You can explain to the president of Delta International why his scheduled plane did not take off on time! Sounds clear enough to me, even if it was spoken in Korean. Their eyes are locked, eyeball to eyeball.

A deadening silence comes over the area. My pilots do not blink. The Korean officials do. "Go, go. Take her and get out of here." We run the length of the corridor and take off with the plane. Truly my angels. Absolute angels! I learn later that Delta International Airlines had made a commitment to pay $50,000 to South Korea if I skipped without producing a passport in Bangkok. A verbal bond had been made by the pilots.

I sit in my seat and feel numb between Korea and Taipei. The pilots are passengers in the business section too. They try to reassure me. Will we have the same problem in Taipei? No, probably not. But Bangkok might be a problem. We land in Taipei. The pilots are right. The airport officials don't like the fact a passenger does not have her passport, but they reluctantly allow me to continue with my guardian angels. They actually smile at me as I walk by. I am feeling a little better. Well, slightly.

As our plane takes off for Bangkok, I look around for my angels and don't see them. My fears surface. Where are my pilots? Who will know about my problem? Questions are streaming through my mind. What is my plan? What are my choices? At this moment, the choices seem far and few between. The numbness sets in again. I close my eyes and struggle to fight the tears back. I finally fall asleep for a few minutes, not long. It feels like someone is watching over me. My pilot angel is standing in the aisle. He smiles and tells me he is glad I am able to sleep a little. I forgot they had told me they would be the pilots on this leg of the trip. I thought they had gotten on another plane, leaving me to fend for myself in Bangkok. Angels don't do that to those in need. These angels are actually flying the plane. A lot of wings are in motion on this flight to Bangkok. My angels are here for the duration.

The pilot tells me there has been no success in finding my passport or even the bag at the San Francisco airport. They have been trying to radio back to the States to track it down. They will keep trying, but there is a communication blackout whenever the plane is near Russia, China or Korea. We may have to wait a little longer, but they promise to keep trying. A feeling of relief overcomes me. At least my angels are still here and I am flying under their protective wings. Things are looking up.

It is a big deal to lose a passport during international travel. The Bangkok officials know me before I even get off the plane. There is a stern looking welcome committee waiting to greet me at the gate. My angel pilots tell me I am in good hands with Robert. He isn't smiling. He escorts me to the Department of Immigration, through customs and everywhere else in the airport. He doesn't leave me for one minute. Well, for a minute. He walks into an office with a glass window and is trying to explain the problem. His eyes never leave me as they look through the window. I am not going to run away, I promise. I am so tired I can't even walk away. He comes out of the office with some documents, but he tells me he will keep them. He has told the airport officials I will be getting a temporary passport from the United States Embassy tomorrow morning. Isn't it *lucky* I have arrived in Bangkok a day early and the offices will be open on Friday? The plan for our lives is in place and we are just living it out now; luck has little to do with it. This particular experience is clearly my choice, but I cannot fathom right now the reason I chose this plan. It is probably a very good thing I did not know what was going to happen in the next moment. If I had known, the outcome of this journey would have been very different and not nearly as significant as it was. I might have opted out and stayed hidden in my home had I known what was in store. This is the easy part of my trip.

Robert's assistant escorts me to the hotel attached to the airport. My travel agent had booked me into this one. Isn't that convenient? What a plan! I am in the hotel registration line and the couple ahead of me are asked for their passports. No one has talked to the clerk about me, at least not in my presence. I approach the counter, but the clerk does not ask me for my passport. She seems to know who I am. Losing a passport during international travel is noticed. Is Big Brother watching my every move?

Thank heavens, or, at the very least, the angels, I have finally gotten to my room. 1:00 a.m. I will take a chance and hope the travel agency in California is open for business. I make the call and Nicole comes on the line. I am crying so hard that she can barely understand what has happened. I am exhausted and know I am not making any sense. Will this crying ever stop? Little do I know this is the easy part of the trip, but, in the moment, it doesn't feel like it. I am asked if I want to return home immediately. No,

I have a commitment to meet the Lama on Christmas Day with Mt. Everest nearby. The mountain is the highest point in the world so I will be at the highest of highs. I will be at the monastery on Christmas Day to meet the Lama. I don't even know the Lama's name. I don't even know why I want to meet him. I don't know if he is a famous Lama or just an ordinary one. I don't know any of that or even know what Lamas do. I just know I am going to be with him on Christmas Day. Nicole is sympathetic. They will try and get a copy of my passport faxed to the hotel before I leave for the United States Embassy. I made a copy, too, but I can't find it. Maybe it is in the overnight bag with the passport and my New Year's Eve dress. Nicole said she would get a copy to me as soon as possible.

It is still dark and there is nothing I can do until morning so I try to sleep for a while. A lot of tossing and turning with intense anxiety. I have no idea what is in store for the rest of the day. I know I have to call the United States Embassy as soon as they open their doors. Can they get me a passport in one day? How much will it cost me? I only have $168 on me. Will my trip to Nepal be canceled? I have to call the airlines and change my flight on Thai Airways. They have me leaving Bangkok this morning. Do they have a flight tomorrow, if I can get my passport? What do I do about my travelers checks? Will American Express come through? Where is their office? The list goes on and on and the tossing and turning continues. Why does everything have to be so hard? I feel so alone.

Daylight is here and there is an envelope under my door. It is a copy of my passport! It has been faxed by the travel agency in America. This should help in getting a new one. There are no coincidences or accidents. My travel agent booked me into Bangkok a day early. I could have flown in on Saturday and then on to Nepal over the weekend. If that had happened, I would have missed the trek completely. I would have had to wait until Monday to get to the Embassy and the Department of Immigration in Bangkok. I would never have been able to catch up with the rest of the Nepal group. Hopefully, without any problems, I will go to the embassy, change my flight schedule, try to replace my traveler's checks and fly to Nepal on Saturday. That will get me there on time. Amazing how the universe revolves with synchronicity, like ripples in the pond - one reaching out and touching the other- events, people and all living things.

I call and change my flight reservation. No problem. I am finally able to get through to the United States Embassy. The lady is pleasant and urges me to show up as soon as possible. I am told to bring four photographs with me along with $65 in United States currency. The copy of my passport will make it easier but it will still take most of the day and I will also have to go to the Thailand Department of Immigration. She will tell me more about that after I arrive.

I decide to take a shower and brush my hair slightly. I put on a little make up, more for the photo than anything else. I am not particularly interested in how I look today. I get dressed and head for the hotel lobby. I just want to straighten out this mess and get to Nepal if I possibly can. I run into one of my pilot angels and I tell him I am headed for the United States Embassy. He wishes me luck. Incredible angels. I appreciate their efforts and belief in me. Men have been helping me in one of my most vulnerable moments. Lessons are coming fast and furious in my direction.

I ask the hotel reservation clerk for transportation downtown to the United States Embassy and I am advised to take the hotel limo service. The limo is nothing more than a small compact car driven by one of the young men. It is going to cost me $29 to go downtown. That is a lot of money for me. I only have $168 on me and $65 has to go for the passport. What is the exchange rate? No, $29 is the amount in US dollars, so I pay and we take off. I didn't know any better. Is my vulnerability still showing?

I know I have to have four photos for my passport. The driver seems like a nice young man. He is talkative, and he agrees to stop by a passport photo shop so I can get my pictures. I am spending several dollars for the photos. The driver seems to be a good friend of the shop owner. They are laughing. The charge seems high, but I am at the driver's mercy so I pay the price.

The driver takes me to the Embassy and tells me he will wait for me. I am grateful he offers. I am in the Embassy and the woman behind the counter seems genuinely sympathetic. She tells me the photos I bought won't work. They are too small and I have to have black and white ones; these are color. The man at the passport shop should have known that. She directs me to another photo shop a few blocks away, and as I leave the Embassy, my driver is nowhere to be found. I had told him I would be a while, and if he wanted to come back in an hour, I might be finished. The clerk tells me the Embassy will be closed for one-and-a-half hours at lunch. I should hurry and get back to the Embassy before they close. They will need that time to issue a new passport to me. The clerk also said I had to report my passport as being lost to the Bangkok Police Department. Without a police report, the Embassy cannot issue a new one. No, don't tell them I lost the passport in San Francisco; just say I don't know where I lost it. It could have been in Portland. After all, I don't know for sure. My Portland airline ticket is stamped, "all legal documents intact," so the reservation clerk may have unintentionally kept my passport.

I am racing along the city street through an unfamiliar city toward the photo shop, and I am not sure where I am going. I find the shop and this man seems to know what he is doing. He knows exactly what I need. He takes my picture and it looks awful. What can I expect going on twenty hours with little sleep and no food. I think the last time I ate was on the plane leaving Portland. Maybe. I am not even sure about that. I'm not sure about anything anymore. Next stop is the Bangkok Police Department. It's easy to find even though it is a few blocks from the Embassy. The clerk has given me good directions. The officer looks at me suspiciously. Where did I lose my passport? I am not sure. I think at the airport. It may have slipped out of my hand. Enough said. I did not say which airport. I think the angels will forgive me for the omission. He issues me a police report. I am racing back to the Embassy and hopefully can get a passport today. The Embassy closes at 11:30 a.m. and reopens at 1:00 p.m. It is 11:15 now. I better run as fast as I can, and I do. I don't know how I am doing this, but intention is everything. It is my intention to get back to the Embassy before 11:30 a.m.

The young driver is waiting for me outside. He went out to get something to eat while he was waiting. I tell him to wait. I'll be back in a minute. I need to find a place to get my traveler's checks replaced; maybe he can help me find a bank. He smiles and tells me he will wait.

The Embassy clerk takes my photos and police report. She has my completed application, the photocopy of the missing passport, and now I have to pay the $65.00. That leaves me with $73.00. I am told to return to the Embassy at 2 p.m. and that my temporary passport will be ready. Then I will have to go to the Thailand Department of Immigration to prove to them I have my passport.

The young cabby is still smiling. He tells me he is going to show me some of the sights, but I say no. I am too tired, but I need to find a bank and then I will buy him lunch for being so nice to me. As we drive away, he tells me that he is charging me $20 an hour, and so far I owe him $60 for the past three hours. He is doing what? I can't believe what I am hearing. No one told me about the extra charges. Is that what limo service means? Boy, did I miss something. This man is taking advantage of me in one of my most vulnerable moments and I am not conscious of it. I open my wallet and naively hand him $60 and ask him to take me back to the Embassy. He asks me for a $5.00 tip; I give him $3.00. I am not thinking clearly. All my defenses are down. After he lets me out, I watch him drive away smiling. I realize I am more angry at me than him. Why would I let him take advantage of me that way? Why would I do that? I suppose because I have done so so many times in the past. When will I finally stop giving pieces of myself away? I still don't know how to figure out who the good guys are. It is different in my work world. My professional judgment is very good. But in my personal world I let men get away with too much and usually at my expense. When am I going to learn?

I shake my head and cry as I stand in the gutter near the sidewalk in downtown Bangkok. When will I learn the lesson? Where is the value I put on myself? Obviously, no one else is going to, if I don't.

It is almost noon and I have to wait until 2 p.m. for my passport. I might as well try and get a cash advance from one of the nearby banks. I am in every bank within a ten block range. No one seems to understand me. Is it my language or my lack of clear thinking? I am crying again. My credit cards don't work at their teller machines. I think I am just having a hard time trying to remember my PIN number and obviously no one else knows it. Why does everything have to be so hard? These banks don't handle American Express. I am told there is a bank a few miles away. I can take the city bus. Not me with my experiences of city buses. Things are hard enough for now.

A cleaning lady at one of the banks brings me a glass of water. She is trying to be an angel. She is an angel, but I am afraid to drink the water. All I need to do is become sick at the Embassy. That would leave an impression. I thank her but don't pick up the glass. It would taste good if I could trust it. Right now, I cannot trust anything. Once again, I try to use the teller machine outside the bank. Nothing is working for me. I have only a few dollars in my purse and I will need money to get to the Department of Immigration. I am still kicking myself for giving all my money to the limo driver. I should have told him what he could do with his bill, but when I am feeling vulnerable that is usually when I let people hurt me the most. It is also the time I give the largest pieces of myself away. What will I learn on this trip? What are the lessons? I am not thinking straight. I haven't been for hours now. Maybe insight will come later. And maybe there are no answers at all. Perhaps it is just a lot of terrible mistakes on a holiday. Maybe it means nothing more or perhaps it means much more than I will ever be able to understand.

I am so hungry. There is a deli across the street from the Embassy. Maybe I can put my lunch fare on a credit card. Just sitting down feels so much better. I order a tuna sandwich and a coke. I don't usually drink cokes, but this is the best tasting drink I have ever had! The tuna sandwich tastes pretty good too. It has been hours since I last ate. My body aches and my energy is gone. I don't know what I will do once I get my passport. The waitress brings the lunch check. She won't take my credit card. She wants only Thai money. I have no Thai money and I don't know the exchange rate;

neither does she. There is another bank next to the deli. She will hold my credit card until I get some Thai money to pay for my tuna sandwich. There are workmen in the lobby redecorating the bank's interior. A lot of construction work is going on. It seems symbolic for the structural and spiritual repairs I am now undergoing. If I believe in symbols and synchronicity, then there are messages and lessons here. But at this very moment, who knows. I am too tired to think about synchronicity right now! I just want to get some money to pay for my tuna sandwich. The teller doesn't understand what I want. It feels like they have never met an American before. None of them seem to speak any English. It would cost too much to exchange a couple of dollars and they won't do it. I guess that is what they are saying.

No one will help me. All I want is some Thai currency. What is so difficult about that? I walk a few steps away from the teller window. I am more than crying. I am sobbing. I can't stop sobbing. I can't walk. I am barely standing. I am shaking. I am a grown woman. I am a doctor. I'm an independent woman who can take care of herself. I should *know* what to do. I don't. Nobody understands me. I am exhausted and can't think this through clearly. Where is the confidence? Where is the self-assured world traveler? I am so vulnerable and so raw. In a foreign land and no one to connect with. I am completely dependent at this moment, and there is no one to depend on. And it simply comes down to knowing that I must pay for my tuna sandwich and that I don't know how to do it by myself.

Another angel appears. Her name is Michele. Maybe she works at the bank. No, she says she is a customer of the bank. All I know is she speaks English. She seems to be a valuable customer to the bank. She and the manager are standing nearby and talking, but she is the one who turns to me with concern on her face. She is in her fifties and well groomed. She places her arms around me. She asks me to sit down and tell her what has happened to me. Little do I know in this moment that I am in the easy part of the trip.

"The first thing we need to do is call American Express. I have the phone number and I will dial it, " she says very gently and firmly. The bank manager shows us to an empty desk and Michele takes over. She speaks English. She and her husband have lived in Bangkok since 1955. She is French but she speaks English beautifully. She places the phone next to my ear and I explain that I am not sure where I lost my checks. Maybe San Francisco or maybe Portland. American Express lives up to their ad. There is a bank at the airport where I can get new checks immediately. The checks are now reported lost. No problem.

Michele escorts me downstairs to the deli. She is going to pay for my tuna sandwich. She then sends me to the Embassy. It is 1:30 p.m. so my passport may be ready. I cross the street and she assures me she will wait at the deli for me. The passport is ready when I arrive at the Embassy. It is temporary for one year. That is fine with me. The photo is awful but I love the cover! I have my passport.

Michele is waiting for me at the deli. She suggests we sit for a few minutes and have a coke and she is going to help me. She will drive me to the Department of Immigration, and she wants to rehearse with me what will happen there. I feel like I am her child patient. I probably am.

She wants me to practice saying "no". Not a little meek "no". A big "NO"! She says she has other things she has to do that afternoon so she cannot stay with me at the Department of Immigration, but she will go as far with me as she can.

"They will try to extort you, Jerri. They will try to get as much money from you as possible. They will try to intimidate you. Just stand your ground, get the document you need, and get out of Thailand and into Nepal. Practice saying "NO", Jerri! Stand your ground. That is what you will have to do with them. Do you understand what I am trying to tell you?"

"Yes, I think so. I will try".

"No, Jerri, don't try. Just learn to say 'NO' clearly and directly. They will understand that. Let's practice as I drive you to the Department. Say 'NO'".

I respond and say "no".

She shakes her head. "I said, say NO"! Learn how to set limits with these people. Don't let anyone take advantage of you. It is very important. Do you understand?

Yes, I understand and I practice saying "NO". Michele nods her head in approval. She said I would need a great deal of patience. If I had seen this day coming, would I have just turned around and gone home the night before? How deep is my commitment to be with the Lama on Christmas Day? I am beginning to wonder. This is an enormous struggle, but in later reflection, it does seem like the easy part of the trip. Little did I know.

The next three hours help me understand patience. I am struck later with how patient everyone seems to be. Michele drives me to the Department of Immigration. She is proud of her new little car and she tells me about it. She just learned to drive a couple of years earlier. Her car is red and she shifts gears as easily as she is teaching me to take care of myself. She has her independence. She has daughters my age. I tell her I am older than she may think. She is surprised by my age. We laugh. I feel like I have aged twenty years in the past twenty hours, but I am feeling better. I continue to practice saying "NO"! She is smiling as she is driving. Her pupil is finally getting it.

Michele hugs me. She gives me her telephone number and extra money for the taxi back to the hotel. She wants to hear me say NO one more time. My "NO" is strong! Michele is happy with my response and she has decided I will be fine. She waves at me as she drives away.

I enter the Department of Immigration building and look for the signs to the right office. Michele has told me which office I will need to get help from. I enter the office and approach the clerk's desk. I tell her I need a document that will allow me to leave Bangkok and go to Nepal tomorrow. She seems to understand me. The clerk spends quite a bit of time on the telephone. First I am weepy. I feel so powerless as my shoulders slump forward and my chest caves in. I know I look like a victim.

Another employee approaches me. She has face cream she wants me to buy. "You are an American," she says. "You have money. Buy my cream." I say NO! She gives me an unpleasant look as she walks away. The other employees don't look very happy either, including the lady at the desk where I am sitting. I hear her mention my name several times on the telephone. Thirty minutes pass and I decide not to sit here any longer with a weepy look on my face. I choose not to be a victim any longer. I am not a victim. I am in my body. I am present. I close my eyes and I begin to meditate. I am instantly with the White Light which is a reflection of the God essence, and I move into a peaceful place.

My thoughts go deeper. Where was I last Christmas? Yes, a significant experience in my life. I was at Macchu Picchu in Peru when Charles and Jerry introduced themselves to me — two single men traveling through Macchu Picchu at Christmas time. We were in a magical, spiritual place and we connected through humor and a common pursuit- our spiritual growth. They asked if I am available for Christmas dinner in Cusco. There was a four hour train ride from Macchu Picchu to Cusco, so they would come to my hotel later that evening, and we could walk to the city plaza and find a restaurant. Traveling alone, especially during the holidays, has always presented the opportunity to connect with new people. That's one of my favorite parts of traveling.

Marcial Boo´ was another friend I met on my travels. We sat next to each other on the train to Cusco. I found myself telling him about people who were so dogmatic and arrogant in their religious beliefs that they determined who would and would not "go" to heaven. If I didn't believe in what they believed I would burn in hell. That was crazy, I told Marcial. As I was talking, Marcial simply and quietly responded, "There is no problem, Jerri." As I continued my tirade at such religious zealots, Marcial speaks again. "There is no problem, Jerri." Eventually I asked what he meant. He replies, "Do you think they are comfortable with their religious beliefs?", and I told him, probably yes. He then asked if I was comfortable with my spiritual beliefs, and again I said yes. Marcial quietly said once again, "There is no problem." Christmas Day 1992 was turning into a unique experience.

That evening Charles, Jerry and I met for dinner. I found myself sitting at a table with two rather straightlaced conservative men who were talking about crystals, auras, and energy. I was amazed at the course of our conversation. Jerry began to tell us about his need to get away from home because his wife of many years had died six months earlier and he could not bear to be at home without her at Christmas. Tears came to his eyes as he talked so lovingly about her. I took a deep breath, because the question I was going to ask was not meant to be rude or insensitive. It was an honest question. I knew logically the answer to the question, but I did not know the answer at my deepest feeling level. This man was showing such feeling. He would know the true answer. It was no accident his name is Jerry. The answer is within Jerry/Jerri.

Gently I leaned across the table and asked, "Was it worth it? Was being married to her all those years worth the pain you are feeling now...was it really worth it?" With tears slowly coming down his face he responded, "God yes, I would be in this much pain every day for the rest of my life to have had the time I had with her. Yes, Jerri, it was worth it." And we all clasped hands and cried together. Connection is worth it. The pain will pass. Love remains, even if that means only in our memory. The loving Light is in and around me as my meditation brings me back to Bangkok, December 1993.

Later I realize my meditation lasted over two hours. My body doesn't move during the meditation and I remain centered in the Light. There is a feeling of calm and it brings me into my own presence and I am completely in my body. Victims usually leave their bodies but I won't do that today. I am emotionally present and I'm not going anywhere else.

In my meditation I note my breathing and move into the emptiness of the experience. It is an opportunity to experience my Beingness. It has been said that prayer is when we talk to God; meditation is when we listen to God. In the moments of silence I become centered, and nothing outside can throw me off center unless I choose to let that happen.

"You must get a new passport! We cannot help you," says a man with a sound of distinct authority. I open my eyes. I am still sitting in the Department of Immigration in Bangkok but with the two hour meditation my light of authority seems to surpass his. I look at the clock on the wall. It is 4:50 pm and it is Friday. I ask him to repeat what he just said. Again he says, "you must get a new passport!" he repeats and he hands mine back to me.

I am now completely behind my eyes which is another way of saying I am fully present in my body and no one is going to violate my space. That won't happen physically, verbally, emotionally and certainly not spiritually. I do not yell or become emotional. I stare calmly back at him and with a solid tone, I say, "This passport is two hours and forty-five minutes old. It is the newest passport you are going to get. Nothing newer!" We stare at each other for a moment. My firmness matches the tone I use when working with divorcing parents who are making unreasonable demands regarding the custody of their children. I am clear and I am present. But my personal life has been different. I have had trouble with the word "no". My masculine energy expresses clearly and sometimes others feel very uncomfortable. What has been missing is being able to express my feminine energy in a soft, nurturing and receptive expression with gentle firmness. There is a time for both, and I need balance. I wonder if I will find that integration on this trip? For this moment, my masculine energy is serving me without the aggressive, attacking mode. The balance is felt by both of us. The male supervisor looks at me. I do not look away. I stare back with the same intensity that I have shown in the past under less vulnerable conditions. The difference is the soft Light that surrounded me through the meditation is still with me and I am at the center of my power. I am safe.

He smiles. "Oh, you just go to the airport tomorrow and they will let you go to Nepal." I ask, "Who are they and what document will they give me so I can go to Nepal?"

"Go see Captain Tik. You will be fine." The man stands up as if he is dismissing me. I remain seated in my chair. "I want you to write the Captain's name on this piece of paper. I want you to write the document he has to give me so I can leave for Nepal tomorrow. I want you to date and sign this paper and I will take it with me. I am not leaving this office until you sign this paper." He continues to stand and I continue to sit. I am not leaving. He must see my Light or must realize I am going to be a permanent fixture in his office through the weekend, if necessary. He sits down and writes the name Captain Tik, a map to his office at the airport, the document he is to give to me, today's date, and his signature, and tells me I can now leave. I tell him, "Yes, now I can leave," as I walk out the door with a smile.

A taxi picks me up outside the Department of Immigration office and charges me $10 for the full trip to the airport hotel. The limo driver had charged me $29 plus $60 plus a $3 tip. Upon my return to the hotel, I walk through the hotel lobby and past the limo counter. The driver is standing there with another employee. The employee yells out from behind the counter, "Lady, you want a ride downtown? We are cheap," and they both laugh. I walk up to the counter, stare at both men and say, "You did something very bad today! You had no right charging me the money you did. You should be ashamed. I have paid the money and I do not expect it back. It is not necessary for me to get it back. You do know about karma, don't you? I believe you do. What goes around, comes around. The money you took today will probably be some of the most expensive money you have ever received. I have no doubt you will remember what I am telling you when you feel you have been cheated, and it will be a much harder lesson for you than it was for me. Trust that. It is the law of the universe." I turned and walked away. It is not my worry whether they heard me. That is not the point. I simply spoke my truth. At some level the universe registered what happened that day and at some point the injustice will be corrected. It is not up to me to find out how. I walk away and they are no longer smiling. It is clear they understand karma.

The Bank of Bangkok at the airport that handles American Express traveler's checks is very cooperative. Yes, they know my checks have been lost. Now I get new checks with little effort. The record is in their computer and they are happy to replace my old ones. Everything has been straightened out. I have met Captain Tik and will have no problem leaving for Nepal tomorrow. I keep my little piece of paper, just in case.

A telephone call to Michele is important. I could not have done this without her. The memory of standing in the bank lobby and sobbing my heart out remains painfully clear. She, like the Delta pilots, has been an angel in every sense of the word. We promise to keep in touch. I must have done something very nice in my past to have such karma come back to me through Michele.

Saturday morning comes abruptly. Captain Tik helps with my transition from Bangkok to Nepal. (Patience is a lesson I am quickly taking in and I arrive at the Bangkok airport one hour early.) I feel like I've already been on a month-long trip. The boarding of the Thai Airways flight goes without incident. Thai Airways has wonderful service. I am sitting in business class and enjoying every minute. As we take off, all I want is to close my eyes and rest. The flight to Nepal will take several hours.

This trip is providing many opportunities to reflect quietly on significant moments of my past and how they are all connected to this trip. The Light is forever present. The angels are nearby. I feel their presence. I find myself reflecting on other difficult and important experiences in my life. The lessons have been significant. My life, perhaps like that of many other people, has been full of struggle. Do we choose, or is it the luck of the draw? Perhaps prior to my birth I decided to get all the lessons I could cram into one lifetime. I wanted to catch up with the many evolved souls who were far ahead on the path of learning and loving. "Throw me everything you have Universe! I want to learn as much as I can and as fast as I can!"

I have had some tough lessons in life and that is what life may bring to each of us. I have learned that life is a process and I get to keep practicing until I get it right. It makes no difference if I make mistakes, as long as I don't keep making the same mistakes over and over. I am also open to the possibility there is no such thing as past lives or future lives but only this moment. I sometimes wonder if time and space are manmade creations formed to accommodate the human body? That thought challenges my frame of reference.

The memories of Bangkok will probably remain in my consciousness for a long time. There have been angels and there have been teachers. I have chosen all of them to be in my life at this time. Even teachers like the limo driver are of value to me. I get to practice keeping the integrity of my soul and working on connection in times of adversity. As the plane flies toward the magical land of Nepal, I continue to learn. I am on my way to meet the Lama and connect with the mountain. The highest of highs is waiting and the angels are calling.

 CHAPTER THREE: **ANGELS ON THE PATH**

We are touching down in Kathmandu. It is a smooth landing and I watch the Nepali people standing behind a fence smiling and waving excitedly. There are many open and friendly faces. I wonder if it has to do with their Buddhist philosophy. I don't know anything about Buddhism, but I am interested in learning. I do know it is a lifestyle as much as a religious philosophy. I once heard it said that the most important thing that has happened to western civilization in this century is the introduction of Buddhism to the West. I'm moved by this insight and my Christian beliefs are not threatened. I remember as a child listening to my father argue with family relatives. He could not believe the majority of the world's population would go to hell simply because they didn't believe a man called Jesus Christ was the world's only savior.

It may all be semantics anyway. Most religions have the same stories and same principles - love and compassion as reflected by people like Gandhi and Jesus. But enough philosophy for now. I must find my ride. I don't even have a name or phone number. Those, too, were in the lost bag.

The passengers are told to stand in the visa line. Some seem familiar with the procedure while others, like me, look completely lost. We have to go from one line to another. I am wishing I could speak more than one language but English is all I know. Oh well, I survived Bangkok! I will survive the Himalayas, too! I have had that feeling of certainty before and it frightens me. Little do I know the most difficult and the most magical parts of this adventure are just beginning.

My backpack seems heavier than I remembered when I left home two days ago. Customs is checking my bags. I have a thirty-pound duffle bag along with my backpack. I have been told, however, the sherpas will be carrying my duffle bag while I carry my backpack on the trek and I am less worried with that knowledge.

A small framed man who is wearing casual clothes approaches me wearing what appears to be a permanent wide grin. "You must be Jerri," he says as he comes toward me. He knows who I am. The driver is also smiling as if he has known me for a long time. Maybe we all have known each other before. Anything is possible today. The guide's name is J.P. Lama. He is the owner of **Guide for All Seasons**, a trekking company in Kathmandu. J.P. and I walk outside toward the van and see Amy who is standing by the van waiting. She's from New York, a strawberry blonde in her thirties, and seems sweet. We laugh as we tell each other we cannot believe we are doing this. She says her family members think she is nuts. I nod. The people I left behind are still shaking their heads with some amusement and a lot of fear. Two single women traveling alone and on an adventure. We have something in common.

Amy is one of the five members of the American trekking team. J.P. tells us he has to go back to the terminal and look for a third member of our group, Ed from Florida. Interesting! We have three corners of the United States represented: California, Florida and New York. I wonder who planned that? I also wonder where the other two people will be coming from? J.P. tells us they are already at the Sherpa lodge in Kathmandu. Ann and Bill are from Washington, D.C., and they arrived earlier in the day.

Obviously Amy and I both like adventure. I tell her I am prone to doing adventuresome things like a tandem jump out of an airplane just so I would know what it felt like to skydive. How much tougher could this trek experience be? I am ready for a new experience. Living life with passion is a choice I willingly make. We continue to wait for Ed, but he doesn't show up. Another traveler problem? I hope not.

J.P. returns to the van and tells us we are going to the lodge without him. J.P. will try and track Ed down after we arrive. Kathmandu is very crowded and dusty. Cattle are wandering aimlessly, while boy-drawn carts race through the narrow stone streets. Scooter bikes weave in and out of the busy traffic. The energy feels different. So many people jamming the streets with cars, cattle and carts. There is no aloneness. People are connecting; they are together walking and talking. We drive past a butcher, sitting under a cotton makeshift tent, cutting up a chicken with parts flying everywhere. This is a common sight throughout the city - vendors selling their wares while sitting on the ground in open air street locations.

The drive to the sherpa lodge is full of unusual sights. The pollution and dust from the road is heavy. I find myself breathing hard as we drive through the streets. The clothes of passersby show western style influence, with the traditional Nepalese dress still present. One can feel the old country presence as well as a new country trying to emerge. Women are wearing the nepalese sari (saari) and many of the men wear the Nepalese tunic (daauraa) on their heads. It must have been a beautiful city once, but now it feels polluted and it is very noisy. Its borders have only been open to westerners for forty years, but the west has certainly made its mark. Everyone seems to be honking their horns.

There is a carefree feeling in the van. J.P. and the driver are enjoying the ride to the Sherpa Lodge and appear to be enjoying each other's company. They attempt to make us feel welcomed. Children play in front of their houses in dirt yards. Old tires rest on the side of the road. I see slogans painted on old buildings, "Vote for tree," "Vote for Sun," and I shake my head in bewilderment. Sure I'll vote for the tree and the sun; sounds like a great alternative to the usual political choices! It is explained to me. The tree is the symbol of the conservative party while the sun represents the communist party. Fascinating symbolism!

The sherpa lodge is a few miles outside the city. As we pull up in the driveway people come out to greet our arrival. Everyone is always smiling. They express such a warmth and genuineness. I wonder again if it has anything to do with their Buddhist philosophy? The younger men carry our luggage upstairs and they are still smiling at us. A lot of good energy fills this house.

It is a four story red brick home with all the modern amenities. Indoor plumbing, a large modern kitchen and a beautiful sunken living room with Oriental carpets and strategically placed art work. I am impressed.

We each have our own bedroom and bath. Our duffle bags are placed in our rooms, but there is no reason to unpack. We will be leaving for the trek after one day of sightseeing in Kathmandu. I look out my bedroom window just in time to see a child squatting down in a field, wiping his rear with a tree leaf as he pulls up his torn pants. Indoor plumbing is still a luxury in Kathmandu.

After I feel settled, I wander downstairs and begin talking with the staff. Santi is a petite, young woman in her twenties and J.P.'s niece. She is the lodge manager, although it appears to be a family affair. Her parents, sisters and brothers and their spouses and children live in the lodge, though on a different floor than the guests. Santi seems always to wear a sweet smile on her radiantly lovely face. She is a new mother, and her parents care for her baby as well as her sister's, while they take care of the guests and the lodge. A gentle young man who appears to be very much in love with Santi, is introduced as her husband. It is obvious he adores her by the expression on his face.

We all have the opportunity to talk and get to know each other. Santi is surprised I live alone. That is unheard of in Nepal. Does my daughter live next door? No, I tell her. She lives about 45 minutes away from me. Does my mother live next door? No, she lives about three hours away from me. Do I have sisters or brothers? I have sisters and they live quite a distance from me too. She is terribly confused. Doesn't all of my family live in the same house? No. We live in different houses and in different cities and even states. It is clearly difficult for Santi to make sense of my lifestyle. I tell Santi, I do have love birds named **True** and **Love**. They keep me company and every night when I walk through the front door, *True Love* greets me. I am laughing and she sees the twinkle in my eye. She laughs too, but she doesn't quite understand the part about me living alone. It is beyond her frame of reference and so it confuses her. Relationships appear to be the most important part of life in Nepal; nothing is more important. She seems to need an explanation as to why the members of my family do not live together but I have none other than the fact that my culture values autonomy, which she doesn't understand. She also doesn't understand my work. Why do people come to my office and talk to me? Why don't they talk to their family when they are upset? We have a different way of living out our lives.

J.P. asks the group if we want to walk to a shrine down the road. "Sure, as long as it isn't too strenuous," I respond. Everyone looks at me and then realizes I am making a joke. Strenuous is the word for the coming two weeks of trekking, not for today. It is a pleasant walk, and we talk and get to know each other along the way. Not so pleasant is the poverty we see. There are no windows on some of the buildings and the children could use baths and new clothing, but, as they laugh and enjoy their games, they seem oblivious to these needs. They look at us with some curiosity, but don't approach us. We are told a school teacher earns an average of $8 a week and that is considered a decent wage. The sherpas who will be trekking with us don't come close to earning that type of salary. How do they survive? Barely, we are told. But it is often easier in the villages. The cost of city living is too high for many Nepalese, especially sherpas.

The visit to the shrine is uneventful. Pleasant, but nothing more. I'm still recovering from the stress of the past two days, so it may take me a while to get in the holiday spirit. Upon our return to the lodge, we are told that dinner will soon be ready so we can clean up and join one another in the dining room. Ed, our missing trekker, shows up during dinner. His plane was not met by J.P. due to a mix-up occurring. Boy, do I know about mix-ups! Ed has finally found us.

The conversation is light and humorous in this young group of trekkers. Ann is an editor, her partner Bill is an attorney, Amy is a financial analyst and Ed is also an attorney. They appear to be in their late thirties or early forties. I hope I fit in. Can a fifty-year-old grandmother keep up with this group, I wonder. I will do my best.

Rice and starches are the primary source of nutrition. The food tastes good, but then the dessert arrives and Bill lets out a "yuck." We begin to laugh. The look on his face says it all. Everyone decides to try it except me. The terrible looks on their faces convince me. I'm not looking for more trouble. We are laughing so loud we are sure we are going to insult the kitchen staff. We try to stifle our laughter, but it is hard to do.

Ed volunteers to turn my wrist watch to Nepalese time. It is a cheap watch, and with synchronicity very present, it is identical to Ed's watch. What is the connection here? He is setting the little hands for a different time zone than where I came from. I notice that the alarm has a pleasant little chime. After Ed sets my watch he sets his own to be **synchronized** with mine and Nepalese time. What does it mean if everything speaks to me? Sometimes I don't know how to interpret its deeper meaning, and this seems to be one of those times. No matter. Maybe it will come later.

I could be fantasizing about Ed, who happens to be a very attractive man. Or perhaps it is just an opening statement that we need to be sensitive to the synchronicity of this trip. Or the universe could be telling me it is late and I'm sleepy. It has been a long day and I do want to turn in early. A thought flashes; it would be nice if Amy and Ed get to know each other. They look like they could go together. She seems, gentle and attractive. He is handsome, masculine and expresses a quiet strength. She may be more willing to have a man in her life at this time. I am really getting used to being on my own and loving every minute of it. I also am completely aware that Divine Order is at work, and meeting my needs and living my truth is all I can ask of myself. Being aware is the important part. Interpretation can create separation which can lead to expectations and I have had enough of those in my life. That isn't a road worth walking.

The electrical adapter fits with my hair dryer. Great, at least I can wash my hair and dry it before the trekking begins. Amy wants to use the adapter, too. We learn to share everything to make it easy on our traveling companions. We share creams and lotions. We share rum for a late night sip. We share hats, snacks and anything that helps one another. I like these people. They are open, friendly and very intelligent. The trek will be meaningful with our connection.

Today is a day of sightseeing. Kathmandu is a fascinating city and the people seem very respectful of one another. The five of us find our way to the spiritual plaza and notice a statue of a former king of Nepal known for placing great emphasis on connection. He believed in unifying people and nations. It was the focus of his kingdom. Aha, I think! Another soul interested in connection.

We see Kumari, the living Goddess, sitting by an open window in an upstairs apartment. Dressed in a bright red sari and wearing a red bow in her hair, she is a five-year-old who has been chosen from hundreds of other little girls to live out the life of the legendary goddess, Kumari. Her body has to be flawless, and she is evaluated through thirty-two mystic virtues criteria. Her horoscope must match the King's, and appointed astrologers confirm this date. She is seen to represent the harmony of Hinduism and Buddhism. It is believed that in past years Kumari was groomed to serve as the concubine to the King. That, hopefully, is no longer true.

We continue the walk through the congested streets of traffic, breathing the terrible polluted air. I have the sniffles, as do some of the others. I have a slight cough, but I also have a lot of energy and am looking forward to Mt. Everest, and the Lama and the monastery. Our guide takes us to the river next. Beside the river is the crematorium where corpses lie on cement tables. A man's arm with his fist closed tightly is lifted in the air above the table. The stench is putrid.

Monkeys run loose all around us and we watch with delight. They don't bother anyone unless food is given, and then they stay close until the food runs out. As we leave the area and walk toward the beautiful city temples, I notice that the city square has many spiritual symbols and buildings. We are walking on the roof of one of the shrines. It is a panoramic view of Kathmandu. The noise and air pollution are very strong, but I can feel the spiritual energy and that feels good.

Tomorrow we will be flying to Lukla which is 9,300' above sea level. It is the base of our beginning climb to the 12,680' high monastery in the Himalayas. Tonight we sit around the fireplace in the sunken living room of the sherpa lodge and get to know each other better. We each have our own reason for coming to the Himalayas during Christmas time. There are those who are at a crossroads in a relationship, their career, and their spiritual journey. I have come on this trip to sort through my separation and connection issues especially with my daughter. We have not spoken for two years, and I miss her terribly. I keep this pain to myself; no one else needs to know.

We have been told the Himalayas are a magical and enchanting place. The unexpected is the only thing we can expect. I know I am ready for that. It has been a long life's journey for me and I am now at this doorstep knowing I will accept the path that is placed before me as I climb to the highest of highs on Christmas Day.

We are in the Kathmandu airport drinking soft drinks, waiting for our flight to Lukla. J.P. will not go with us. Nima, our head guide, is in Lukla waiting for us. Sherap, the second sherpa in command, will fly with us to Lukla. He is a gentle looking young man, perhaps in his early thirties, certainly no older. He is clean shaven and dresses neatly. He is about 6 feet in height and he is lean, probably from all the trekking he does in the Himalayas. He smiles shyly when J.P. introduces us to one another, but his eyes are steady and clear, and I know there is a unspoken depth to this man.

Our plane is small and the trip blissfully uneventful. Sherap sits directly in front of me in the narrow seats of the propeller driven plane. He seems to be leading me from the beginning. Clouds surround us as we descend toward the mountains. Oops! We are suddenly landing. This is the shortest runway I have ever been on. Mountains surround us. Amy and I look at each other and share a nervous laugh. Our stomachs were left back behind the clouds. But now we are here and it looks like we are ready for the adventure of our lives. Expect the unexpected, they say. So I do.

Nima and the other sherpas meet our airplane while Sherap helps us off the plane, one at a time. He has a spiritual quality that is obvious from the moment I meet him.

We are shown to the dining room. It's very cold, and I continue to wear my parka while eating the heavy rice dish with curry seasonings. Hmmm! My maiden name is Curry. I wonder if there is a significance. I have always liked curry seasoning. A client recently told me she liked the name Curry; for her it conjured up a feeling of being nurtured. I also like the name Curry, so I probably will drop my married name altogether once I get back to the United States.

The rice, along with all the other starches we are getting, should fortify us throughout the trek. I am told oatmeal is particularly popular in the sherpa lodges. Good. I like oatmeal. The lodge seems fairly modern and reminds me of a ski chalet dining room, but without the surrounding snow. It's December and we are at 9,300'. I am glad there is no snow. I was told by the travel agent snow would be unlikely, but at that time it was difficult for me to believe. I am used to seeing snow at 9,300 feet in the winter, but this is a very different place. I don't know how dissimilar it is to what I know yet; it just feels and looks very different.

Nima tells us we might have a chance to meet the high Lama; he will do what he can to give us that opportunity. I am puzzled. I silently think to myself, "Of course, I am going to meet the high Lama!" It will be on Christmas day. I have never had any doubt. I wonder when and where I became so certain of that fact?

The others have started walking. I am still in the lodge trying to stay warm. Sherap suggests we move out with the others. Sure. That is why I'm here. I have my walking sticks. It was a questionable investment, but the man at the sports shop strongly recommended them. They can be adjusted to different heights depending on the terrain, like ski poles. Sherap asks if I need to have them adjusted. Yes, they need to be lengthened. Afterward, we begin our climb. The path is narrow and the air chilly. Within thirty minutes, Sherap and I both know I can no longer carry my backpack. Sherap volunteers to carry it for me, and I am thankful. I could not go on with it. This is the first of many times I say to myself, what would I do without Sherap? He smiles as if he is reading my mind. We are closely connected, and I wonder what the feeling is about. He is very sweet and he is very young.

Our first day will be four hours of climbing to Phakding (8,875') where we will spend our first night in a sherpa lodge. I am confused with the change in altitude. Are we going down the mountain? No, Sherap assures me. We will be climbing up and down throughout the trip. Sherap tells me about his wife, an English school teacher, and his two-year-old daughter, Dicki. Sherap speaks excellent English. He tells me his parents live in Bhutan and that the one request he would have is in his next life to come back again as their son. We smile at each other. There is a lot of love in this man. He stays so clean and neat despite all of the dust and dirt on the path. I wonder how he does it but I am too shy to ask.

It is a pleasant walk and Ed slows down to join us. When Sherap tells us he wants to come to the United States, Ed and I look at each other and smile. We mention the crime rate and how bad it is in our country. Sherap doesn't seem to understand. He still wants to come.

I talk about my philosophy which is that all things are connected. Synchronicity exists, I say — like ripples in a pond, one reaching out and touching the other; simultaneous interconnection of all things. I think there is a direct connection between our high crime rate and the fact that our country is the largest exporter of weapons and arms in the world. The old mirror philosophy: what we see is what we are, and what we do to others is what we will experience ourselves. Also, if we stay stuck in our fear, that fear may become our reality. Ed listens. Perhaps the new thought expands his frame of reference. We talk about transitions in his life. He has decisions to make about quitting a job and taking another with more job risks, but with possibly more rewards. He hopes the challenge of the climb will release his fear so he'll make a decision.

The climb is getting harder and the talking stops. I need to breathe deeply as we move up the mountain. The terrain appears to be getting more rugged with every step. Quiet steps and quiet moments; we each are in our own place of deeper thoughts.

My thoughts drift back to Mt. Shasta, in 1984. It's been ten years but it seems like a lifetime ago. Maybe it is because so much has happened since then. A woman I know by the name of Josephine Taylor, lives at the base of Mount Shasta. She is 105 years old now. I met her when she was 91. She seemed to talk above my head, or certainly not within my frame of reference at that time. I seldom knew what she was saying, but I would get important pieces, like the time she talked about finding a new star. Years later astronomers confirmed the star and the location. She also talked about "cleaning up the earth". Cleaning included fires, rains, and other natural disasters. She said the negativity was being pushed out but there would be many struggles until it was completely gone. She never charged any money to share her teachings. She said she was a clerk for God and it was her job to share spiritual information for all those who were willing to listen.

Josephine taught me about automatic writing. She said, for most people, the calling usually occurred about 3 a.m. I told her I often woke up at that time and didn't know what to do with myself. She suggested I have a note pad and pen nearby and begin to write, after surrounding myself in the White Light. Then I was to write the name of a guide, and the words would flow from there. When I told her I didn't know any guide, she asked me to close my eyes and speak the first name that came to me. I immediately said, "David". I told her I remember waking up in the middle of the night as a child quietly calling the name "David". I never knew a David in my family. I just knew the name evoked a heartfelt connection for me as a small child. I was very young when David came into my consciousness. Many years later, as an adult, I learned of the greater significance of the spiritual teachings related to David. David is the great-grandfather of all Native American Indians, and Jewish beliefs place great importance on the symbolism of David. Even though I knew biblical stories, it wasn't until later that I learned of the Holy Bible Revelation scriptures:

"And to the angel of the church in Philadelphia write: These things saith he that is holy, he that is true, he that hath the key of David, he that openeth, and no man shutteth; and shutteth, and no man openeth." (The Holy Bible, Revelations 317).

"Jesus have sent mine angel to testify unto you these things in the churches. I am the root and the offspring of David, and the bright and morning star." (The Holy Bible, Revelations 22.16)[1]

My awareness returns to the Himalayas and the present. I look around and find that Ed has moved far ahead and out of sight. He may have caught up with the others on the trail. Sherap guides gently, but we don't speak. He is sensitive to my needs. He asks me if my walking sticks are the right height for the terrain, and adjusts them frequently as we climb. The energy is one of harmony all around me. We continue to climb and I am moving deeper into my thoughts of the past. Josephine has guided me also. She said it was possible that the Holy Bible was written through automatic writing. Interesting thought. She guided me in learning automatic writing and one of my first writings reflected the words,

"The skies open; do so with your eyes, your mind and your heart. Give all you can and be rewarded in kind. Joy is yours to give among all. Teach my words. I renew your strength. Life began as One. We are still one but scattered to choose freely. Bring together my family from all parts of the

world. Do so through love and the written word. Find your place of solitary peace and write all that I give you. Your guides will feed you, nourish your mind, give peace to your soul. Begin this week. All you meet, show unconditional love. Do not judge and show no bitterness. My example will be enough. Continue to remember the Redwoods. My words will comfort you. Remember all souls in the shells are living on different levels. You know not what is in their hearts or minds. Live with God. Live on the spiritual level and all you deserve will be yours. Cause no suffering among men. Harm no being with anger or bitterness. Love gently. My example must reach the people through you, my child. Each angry word closes the door to a human heart. Open the door and let me lead the way. Compassion and understanding come from us before it can reach others. Be true and express your feelings, but do not create sadness and hurt. Be gentle in your words, your thoughts, and your deeds. Your words will be long remembered and My creation will be fulfilled."

Later that year, on May 5, 1984, I traveled to Mt. Shasta after a specific automatic writing experience directed me to the mountain on that day. Mt. Shasta is one of the tallest mountains in the western hemisphere. It has such a regal elegance. I wonder if Mt. Everest is as regal? Everest is twice as high, so regal seems the proper word. It must be a magnificent mountain, and to be near it on Christmas Day has to be an exceptional high. But that is the future, and my mind once again begins to reflect on the past.

My writing directed me to Mt. Shasta and said I can ask God any ten questions I wished to ask and that I will receive the answers. I would also meet a young woman named Sandy who was a teacher for me. After checking in to my cabin at Stewart Mineral Springs, I drove to town to have dinner with two friends, Donna, a practicing Buddhist, and Dorothy, the owner of a metaphysical bookstore in town. Throughout the meal I was asking everyone I met if their name was Sandy. Dorothy told me to let it go, and then it would come in. She was right, and I did let it go. We had more conversation and Dorothy asked me if she could accompany me to the top of Mt. Shasta the next day. She assured me she wouldn't bother me while I was asking my questions of the Universe. Of course! I would enjoy the company.

We left the restaurant and I drove back to my place. I stopped by my friend Paula's cabin on the way. I wanted to return an audio cassette she had loaned to me.

"Come on in, Jerri. I want you to meet a friend," Paula said with a tone that suggested she would not take "no" for an answer. I agreed, but said, "Only for a moment," because I was very tired. I was looking forward to starting my little wood stove, meditating for a few minutes and then reading myself to sleep, which would not take long.

We walked into the kitchen where her friend was doing the dishes. Paula introduced me to Sondra, and we greeted each other casually. We sat at the table and began to discuss our spiritual beliefs and growth. Paula's friend was an extremely insightful individual. I was learning a lot from her. Then the light bulb goes off! I say, "you are Sandy... I mean Sondra... I didn't get it with the pronunciation." She laughed nervously, as did Paula. "Some people refer to me as Sandy but I prefer Sondra". I explained my automatic writing experience which talked about meeting Sandy, and we all laughed together. She then gave me her business card. Behind her name were the initials, F.G.M. I asked for the meaning, and she said, "Fairy God Mother." We laughed again. Eventually I said goodnight and went to my cabin for a quiet and peaceful sleep.

The next day, Dorothy and I drove up to Mt. Shasta. Mt. Shasta had some very easy paths. Dorothy went off on her own. I managed to find the specific location that was described in my writing. A circle of trees with a rock formation nearby, and a stream of many diversions. The questions were emerging in my mind. I trusted they would be exactly as intended. The Voice impression indicated it was not an earthshaking event that day but that my being on the mountain was one small step of faith on my journey toward enlightenment. I am beginning to remember my questions and the answers as my Himalayan trek continues.

1) How was the world created?

Answer: *"Synchronicity,"* emerges from the inner voice. I think to myself what does that word mean? A response: *"Like ripples in a pond, one reaching out touching the other."*

2) What is the purpose of life?

Answer: *"So all living beings will evolve to the God state and be One with me."*

3) Is there life on other planets comparable to our own?

Answer: *"Yes."*

4) Will man destroy man?

Answer: *"Man may destroy man. Man will never destroy life."*

5) What is my function on this planet?

Answer: *"To be a faithful teacher."*

6) How can I best serve God?

Answer: *"Be your full potential. Teach the way you know to be truth."*

7) Who will join me on the spiritual path and what will be our calling?

Answer: *"You know those who join you. They each will receive their own directive. You know yours as has been told."*

8) What does directive mean?

Answer: *"Inner guidance through the Light."*

9) How can we perpetuate the spiritual awareness so all humankind can benefit from your love and wisdom?

Answer: *"Live in each person's shoes when you feel conflict. Be my example in all you think, say and do, and have compassion toward every creation you come in contact with in the universe."*

10) What part of the Master Plan will I be serving?

Answer: *"An insignificant part, according to universal terms, but a significant part, according to My terms."*

I knelt and quietly expressed my appreciation for the connection and wisdom. I felt blessed.

I returned to the car and soon Dorothy joined me. We got in the car but it wouldn't start. It was shortly before noon. I had a CB radio in the trunk and I tried to use it. I yelled into the speaker, hoping someone would hear my distress. "We are stuck up here on Mt. Shasta. Can someone get a tow truck for us?" I yelled that over and over for several minutes.

Dorothy and I looked at each other and began to laugh. She told me her friend Gladys often drove up to the mountain and Dorothy said, "Wouldn't it be great if we saw her?" Just as she said that, Gladys drove around the corner! She stopped and we met. She would take my roadside service card to the gas station in town and have the tow truck come and get us. We appreciated the effort.

Gladys drove away and we continued to wait. A lone man drove up and stopped his car. He had heard us on the CB radio and decided to come and see if he could help. He began to talk about his personal losses during that past year. His wife had died a year earlier and his only son, a grown man, had died six months later. He was in tremendous pain. Rightfully so, since separation is the hardest lesson in life.

We talked for over thirty minutes. He cried and we cried with him. He was beginning to feel better when the tow truck and Bruce, the driver, arrived. Harold, our visitor, assured me he would be all right. I gave him some names of people who might know someone who could help him. He appeared to be comforted from our time together.

"There is no hope," Bruce said as he slammed down the hood of the car. He then hooked the car up to the tow truck and told Dorothy and I to get in for the ride back to town. We hugged Harold and told him to stay in touch. As we drove down the mountain, I felt the vibration of the mountain deeply. It felt like waves moving through me. The mountain was connecting me with the voice impression. I spontaneously yelled, "Oh, stop!" I forgot. My writing told me I could not leave the mountain until after 1 p.m., and it is one o'clock. The car would start, I was sure. We could leave on our own.

Bruce looked at me, and with frustration had said, "Do you want to get out here or what, lady?". Dorothy told me not everyone in Mt. Shasta City thought the way we did, so why didn't we just go down the mountain with him. I smiled, nodded and closed my eyes. The driver didn't look too happy about my comments. We pulled in to the station just as Donna drove up to buy gas. I thought, isn't synchronicity wonderful!

Bruce unhooked the chains from the car. I told him the car would start, and he began to argue with me. I smiled with certainty and placed the key in the ignition. The car turned over immediately. Donna and Dorothy smiled with me as Bruce walked away scratching his head. It was silly for me to forget that part of the writing.

Is my certainty lacking as I continue my climb in the present? The climb is rough. Rougher than I thought it would be. In fact, I don't remember even thinking it would be rough; rather, I thought it would be an adventure with beautiful scenery and a Lama to meet on Christmas Day. I am learning, however, that this trip is not exactly a walk in the park. The climb is becoming more difficult step by step.

My goal is to reach the mountain top. There are words floating in and out of my thoughts. The words turn in to music. The melody seems to get louder and louder as the journey becomes more challenging. As hard as it may seem at this very moment, there is always something good in everything I see, and *I do believe in Angels*. There is a song to sing and the melody is racing through my mind. The words become one with the gentle breeze blowing through the branches of the trees.

It reminds me of a song that I had heard several years earlier. The song is called **I have a Dream** sung by ABBA.[2]

I have a dream as I continue the climb. Now my dream is to reach the mountain top and meet his Holiness, the Lama.

The music resonates to my experiences of the past year, especially now. The words *"...to help me cope with anything"* are becoming more apparent with every step I take.

We have just reached a small village, and I am coughing up some phlegm but there is no reason to mention it. I am dragging. Perhaps the others notice. Sherap and I have finally arrived. He looks clean and calm. He always does. The others look relaxed and rested. They have waited for us and have been drinking hot tea for quite some time. I must have been at least forty-five minutes behind them for most of the morning. They assure me they don't mind waiting. Nima has been busy preparing a simple snack and it will be ready soon. Nima will prepare all of our food. He is very careful and clean and he seems to take great care in nurturing us. Dysentery is a real fear for American soft stomachs. I wish I could get to know the others better, but I just can't seem to keep up with them. Well, those are my limits and I have to learn to accept them. Life seems to be a struggle for me; at least, it has been. I hope that will change but the truth is, I don't know any other way of being.

The hot lemon tea tastes good. The air has a chill to it when we are still, but not as we make the strenuous climb. I haven't needed to wear my parka since leaving Lukla, nor have I needed my gloves, but I have worn my knit cap to keep my ears warm. My thermal underwear, wool slacks and wool sweater seem to be enough for daytime. I wonder, though, what will the night bring? We are told it will be below freezing, but there won't be snow. We will be able to see it, but we won't be in it. There could be a storm, but it's not likely.

The villagers watch us carefully as they pass by. Children are near, and I remember the colorful rainbow and angel stickers I have in my pocket. I pull them out and the children clamor around me. I pat a sticker on the hand or cheek of each child, and they smile in delight. They love the stickers, and it is much better than candy or gum. It is wonderful that these simple things please them. I hope they don't lose their appreciation for simple joys, but progress may someday cause that to happen. For now, it feels like it will be a very long time before western progress invades these villages, something with both positive and negative consequences. As I look out over the mountains, I wonder how much progress we really need. These people seem very happy. Maybe they have progressed more than we have. They certainly appear to have their priorities in the right place, valuing relationships above all. Here I am learning about relationships again. What more will I discover as we climb?

We begin our trek again, planning to walk another two hours today. The scenery is beautiful. The majestic mountains surround us and the paths are picturesque, composed of silky, light-colored dirt beneath our feet. When we walk, the dirt kicks up slightly, like angel dust. It has a soft and wispy feel. On the trail, the yaks move us out of the way. I've needed to get off the narrow trail several times as the cattle and their owners came ambling by. The loads these villagers carry on their own backs are amazing. The people and the yaks are the only form of transportation available to bring in lumber, water and food to the villages. The trails are too steep for carts. Most of the people have never even seen an automobile. Their frame of reference doesn't allow for automobiles, computers, fax machines, and all the things we take for granted in the western world. They are wearing sandals and cotton shirts without coats, and they climb with certainty over the sharp rocks. The rough terrain doesn't seem so to them, as they walk these paths daily.

I have been sniffling and coughing up phlegm almost all day. The phlegm is looking pretty green, but there is nothing I can do about it now, so I just try to keep my lungs as clear as I can. There doesn't seem to be any reason to mention my cold to anyone. What could they do? When we are stopped on the path by some villagers with a sick infant who are looking for medicine, Sherap tells them they will have to go to Shyangboche; it is the only place in the area with a doctor. They know, but think it is too far to go with the baby. They will continue to try their own remedies. They thank us as we continue our climb.

I am still coughing, but I am far enough back on the trail so no one notices and if Sherap does, he isn't talking about it. If I have to cough at night, I decide, I will cough into the pillow so no one will hear me. Step after step, I continue the climb.

The Phakding sherpa lodge appears out of nowhere! Phew! It feels as though we have been climbing most of the day. The lodge is a wooden rustic building with a wood burning stove in the center of the common room. Amy and I have decided to share a sleep cubicle, because it seems large enough. I am ready for a good night's rest.

They have given us each a bucket so we can have a private "inhouse" rather than traveling to an outhouse late at night without any lights to guide us. We are drinking a lot of liquids on the trail as it is very important to avoid dehydration.

For now it is still afternoon and the children in the lodge watch us with curiosity. They are always smiling, it seems, and have a luminous light in their eyes. The rainbow and angel stickers are popular with them, and they get excited as I pass some out. Nima finally announces dinner is ready so the children leave the common room and the sherpas bring our dinner to us. It is a sauce with rice.

All of the sherpas are small-framed men. Sherap is the tallest at 6'; the others appear to be no more than 5'5". All of them weigh a lot less than I do, but they must be very strong to climb the mountain carrying three or four duffle bags that weigh thirty pounds each. Whenever they enter the common room they smile shyly and apologize for disturbing us. They are very sensitive and polite people.

Our English dialogue prevents some of the sherpas from joining in. They speak only Nepalese but they, too, smile a lot. We are all gathered around the wood burning stove. As night begins to fall, the chill becomes noticeable almost immediately. We five Americans are kindred spirits. We laugh easily, and share moments of emotional openness and intimacy through our conversations. The wood burning stove is a popular hangout. The sherpas stand around for a time, but eventually disappear into the kitchen with Nima. We are the last trekking group of the season. Blizzards in this part of the Himalayas will begin in January.

The innkeeper uses pine cones to keep the lodge warm. Heavy burning wood is hard to come by in the mountains. Nima tells us we will see the sacred Buddhist prayer walls, several villages and well-terraced hillsides. We will also see the sacred mountain of Khumbila (18,800'), which remains virgin, at least from climbers. Sacred mountains cannot be climbed, and Khumbila is considered the protector deity of Tibetan Buddhists. We will be in Sagarmatha, the first national park in the Himalayas for a large part of the trekking experience. On our travels, we will cross swing bridges and cross the Dudh Kosi river. Swing bridges are not sturdy, but Nima assures us the yaks walk on them so the bridges will hold us too.

Nima wants us to tell him if we begin having headaches or nausea because we may be getting altitude sickness, which can be very dangerous. It can cause death, says Nima, and he will have to take us off the mountain if we get sick. I am confident I won't get those symptoms because I am taking the medicine prescribed by my doctor. I started in Bangkok. No need to mention it to anyone. I just know I won't get sick.

Amy and I are still laughing about the potty buckets. We decide to put a plastic bag over it to cut the odor. During the night, with the cubicles so close, we hear tinkling hitting the buckets, and we giggle to each other again. I am wearing my wool cap, my gloves, thermal underwear and wool scottish plaid pjs my mother and stepfather bought me for the trip. They are very warm and come in handy.

The sherpas will bring a bowl of hot water for each of us as the morning wake up call comes. We are warned we must take advantage of the hot water immediately, or it will be cool within minutes. Our sponge baths will be limited, but I think back to my first option of sleeping in a tent, and realize what a luxury having a bowl of hot water is on this trip. The wooden bed slats are also preferable to sleeping on the ground, so overall the universe is looking out for my best interests, or maybe it just knows my limitations.

We spend a layover night at the lodge. The day is for day hikes. I stay in so I can shake this cough and congestion. Amy, Ann, Bill and Ed take off on a hike. Maybe if I was in my thirties again I would be joining them, but then I also know there must be plenty of fifty-year-olds who are doing just fine on their Himalaya treks. It was so cold last night in the cubicle that Amy and I decide to sleep in the common room tonight. I am glad we are staying at the lodge longer.

I am enjoying the trek, but it is much more challenging than I ever imagined. I wasn't expecting mountain climbing, and that is what this feels like to me. The sniffles aren't helping me keep my strength up, but I am taking cold tablets to manage the congestion. So much stress on me in Bangkok I am now developing two fever blisters on my lips. Terrific! Not only do I feel sick, but now I look sick, especially if these blisters run their full course. I won't be winning any beauty contests on this trip. No cream or make-up to help hide the sores, and they hurt. Well, maybe a good night's sleep will help me regain my strength. Tomorrow will come early, so I turn in for the night. I find myself coughing into my pillow so I won't disturb the others.

Today we are climbing to Namache Bazaar at an altitude of 11,300'. It is an early morning call. Nima tells us we will be trekking about eight hours and climbing 3000' feet. That is twice as long as we have already trekked. Sounds like it may be rough, but my resolve is firm. I'll be fine. I have rested and my cough seems to be calming down. The phlegm isn't as green and ugly as yesterday. Just a little is coming up, so I should be all right. It is the Wednesday before Christmas, 1993, and I will be at the monastery on Christmas Day to meet the Lama. That I know with all my heart and soul.

As the walk becomes more strenuous, the challenge exceeds even my imagination. I am now beginning to wonder if I really can keep up. My doubts are coming fast and frequently. I keep stopping to try to breathe. My breathing is shallow, and I feel faint as I try to take air into my stomach. I am now on all fours, trying desperately to grip my way up the side of the mountain. The river is running swiftly alongside of us and the river can be heard throughout the canyon. The yaks come by on the narrow trails and don't stop for us. It is my job to get out of their way. Villagers smile as they watch me grab branches and rocks to hold on while they pass by. My walking sticks come in handy most of the time, but some of the time I am just trying to crawl my way up the mountain. I didn't bring good gloves, and my hands are getting scratched. My clothes are dusty and beginning to smell pretty bad. Sherap looks neat and clean. I still can't figure out how he does it.

We stop for lunch. While waiting for Nima to prepare it, I decide to sit by a little creek running alongside the roadside inn. The water quietly ripples over the small rocks in the stream, and as my hand swirls through the water, I am thinking about the energy of this beautiful, spiritual place. The yaks are walking very near me now, and I no longer stand or move away. I simply don't feel afraid any more. Maybe it is simply the way I look at things. One minute they are yaks and scaring me; the next, they are simply cows and wandering by doing their own thing. This feels like a land without fear.

I feel at peace as I am in a very peaceful, though challenging, place. Do challenge and peace go together? I suppose so, because I am feeling both right now. I also feel full after the meal. The food is good, and again we begin the trek.

The group moves out fast, and again I fall behind. Sherap stays near me as the second part of the day begins. I feel at peace, but also physically exhausted. The villagers look as dusty as I do but then they have been here a lot longer than me. The trail becomes rough almost immediately. The villagers don't seem to notice the difficult terrain. They aren't crawling through the dust the way I have been doing for most of the day. This is not easy and I am wondering why I have chosen another struggle in my life.

I can hardly breathe. I am now coughing up lots of green phlegm with blood and I feel dizzy and "spacey," almost like I keep leaving this uncooperative body. Victims leave their bodies; I don't do that anymore. I keep talking to myself: "stay present, Jerri. Stay here. Breathe deeply. Feel my body. Stay in my body." I come back and I cough up more blood and phlegm. I have to keep going, but I don't know how. Foolishly I

think maybe I am coughing up blood because I am straining my chest muscles from coughing so much. I am rationalizing madly so I can do what I feel I need to do. I must get to the monastery and meet the Lama on Christmas Day! I still don't know what Lamas do, but that doesn't seem important.

As I slowly crawl on the upward dusty path, I remember I've often taught children powerful visualizations. Maybe I should create one for myself as I climb. I need all the help I can get.

Within my mind's eye I see a little angel with green wings inside my lungs. She has a shovel, and is shoveling out the fluid from my lungs as fast as she can so I can breathe. She is working so hard she is perspiring, so she wipes her forehead and leans against her shovel. She calls in another little angel who also has green wings. Colors are significant and they have specific interpretations for me. Green is a healing color, just as pink is a color symbolizing love. Both angels are shoveling as fast as they possibly can. Now I see two little angels with white wings, one on each shoulder, pushing me up the mountain as their wings flutter and flap in the wind. They, too, are out of breath, but still they continue. The little angels are working hard to get me to the top of the mountain, to the monastery so I can meet the Lama on Christmas Day. I begin to see a white satin cord tied around my waist, pulling me to the top of the mountain. I see it as plainly as the brush branch protruding on the path. It is a beautiful white satin cord and possesses unspeakable strength. The angels are committed and they are wonderful. They are doing most of the work, and we climb together for hours. They help me to succeed in my mission by staying with me and providing some of their will when I feel I have none left of my own. Tears come to my eyes and they are instantly wiped away. It is so hard climbing this mountain, but I know we will do it. I believe in angels and they are with me in this moment.

Eventually we come to a flat part of the trail. We are no longer climbing, and I am resting as much as I can. So are my angels. I am also trying to breath deeply and evenly. As I turn the corner, there is Sherap waiting for me on a rock ledge. His eyes are closed. He is in deep meditation. I stop and silently wait for him. I am given an opportunity to pray in this quiet moment. Our eyes open at the same moment and we tilt our heads toward one another in the Buddhist tradition. He tells me we only have a couple of hours until we reach the lodge.

I turn to my right and see the river and canyon below. Sherap has my backpack, which contains my paper disposable camera. I ask for the camera, and then aim it in the direction from which we have just come. The picture is taken, and as I turn to my left, I glance at Sherap and we smile with a look of knowing, but consciously we don't know what we know. I don't know what we are saying with our mutual smiles, but it seems special in this moment. It is as if our souls are touching in a genuine and tender mystical moment that we cannot describe with words. The feeling of connection is present and the knowing, is not conscious. We continue the climb and the angels encircled with rainbows are with us.[3]

The coughing continues and the blood is still here. No one is watching me except maybe Sherap from time to time. I continue climbing — on all fours again at many times, but the angels and satin cord are helping me every inch of the way. My leg muscles are beginning to experience spasms and my shoulders are tight. My hands are sore from holding on to the sticks too hard and from climbing over the rocks. I am trying to climb the easiest way I can. From time to time I am directly behind Sherap, and I carefully follow his tracks. He must be taking the easiest steps up this mountain. Boulders are in the way and the trail narrows frequently. I will do what he does. He looks at me with concern, but nothing is said. We keep climbing. Villagers pass me and give me glances. I am struggling harder physically than I ever have in my life. Getting hit by a bus was easy compared with what I am going through now. The emotional struggles that I've experienced in my life are more comparable to this climb. Both are tough, and I cannot decide which has been tougher. Why does life have to be so hard?

Before leaving the United States, I remember telling my friends as they looked at me skeptically, "It isn't like I am going to be climbing up the side of a mountain full of rocks." Now I understand their looks. The rocks are big and hard and everywhere.

Magical and musical words continue to float in and out of my consciousness. We are crossing a swing bridge and the roar of the river below reminds me; as I cross the stream, this is my dream.

My dream is to meet the Lama. I don't know why. What could be so important? I don't know why, but I do know it is *very* important. Dusk has arrived and we are now at Namache. Majestic Mt. Everest sits in the background. She is beautiful and she is regal. The highest point in the world, this snowcapped mountain is a sight to see. Mother nature at its finest, and truly unconquerable. Man is not nearly big enough. At least not physically. At least not me. I am very sick and my legs can barely carry me up the steps to the lodge. I silently wish the lodge was on flat land, but we have a few steps to walk up. I don't know if I can climb the steps. The angels nudge me on.

The others are resting in the common room. It appears it was a hard day for them, too, but perhaps not as hard as it was on the oldest member of the group. I thought I would have the stamina for this trip. Now I just don't know if I can go on. Nima tells us we will be here for two nights. Great! Maybe I will be able to rest enough to continue on. I want to go to the top. I really want to be with the Lama on Christmas Day. Nima tells us he is still not sure he can arrange a meeting, but he will try once we get to Tengboche Monastery on Christmas Eve day. I know silently we are going to meet the Lama. The plan is in place and far beyond anyone changing it now. We will meet. I know that with all my heart and soul. I don't know how I know. I just know.

Dinner arrives around the wood burning stove in the common room and I push most of it away. I cannot eat very much even though I know I need the strength. I can barely breathe. We all decide to put our sleeping bags in the common room and sleep around the stove tonight. I need as much warmth as I can get, so I am willing to join the group tonight. I am sitting on the cushioned seat ledge drinking a cup of hot apple cider. It is a luxury, and I am enjoying every sip. A little kitten wanders by. I reach out and pet it gently and it climbs into my lap. I have found a friend for the night as the kitten snuggles up to stay warm against my clothing and sleeping bag. As the group conversation turns to "cats," I say, "I think I am in my eighth life. I still have one more to go this time around." We laugh. The kitten and I become friends until the early morning hours when it jumps off my bag and leaves quietly.

Christmas is two days from now. I remember another Christmas, December 25, 1989. Four days earlier my third divorce had been finalized. It was an extremely painful time. Staying in the same town as my former husband and his new family was too hard, so I gave up everything and moved to another city. I think most women do that; maybe a lot of men do it too. Had I done the right thing? Should I have stayed and fought harder to keep my old life? My inner voice said I had chosen correctly.

I was hanging pictures in my new home on Christmas Day. My parents had come by earlier and asked me to join them with relatives. I declined; I wanted to be in my new home and with me.

My mother and stepfather wished me a happy Christmas and left. My radio was on as I was hammering nails in the walls to hang pictures and a man's voice came on the air. He began to tell the story of the **Happy Prince**.[4] I had not heard it in forty years.

It was a story that brought back many memories. When I was ten years old I sat with my family around the dinner table telling them the story of the **Happy Prince**. A statue and little swallow meet and spend the winter giving away the jewels and gold adorned by the prince. Eventually they realize they have given too much of themselves in order to help others, but they are recognized by God as being the most precious ones on earth. My parents and sisters sat around the table crying when they heard the story.

In 1989, as I listened to the radio, I sat on my couch and wept quietly. My life had come full circle. Had I been anywhere else, I would not have had the gift of listening to the precious and gentle story. I was in the right place at the right time on Christmas Day, 1989. Synchronicity once again. Now I could put my childhood issues, such as watching my father self-destruct through alcoholism, behind me. As an adult, I had familiar patterns with men. Now I was no longer willing to be in a world of pretend or denial; as if everything was fine. I had given too many pieces of me away or been expected to give away. When I realized there wasn't much left to give, I left. It wasn't where I belonged anymore. I belonged right here in my new life. A church I had attended off and on for eighteen years was near and I knew the integrity of my soul would be regained. It had been a painful time, but the grieving would end, the healing had begun and I was on my path toward wholeness.

And this is another Christmas. It is 1993 in the Himalayas. My life has been fulfilling for the past few years. I am on the right path and have been for some time now. The inner voice may not always seem logical, but it is always right. I am thankful for having honored my inner voice. I fall asleep knowing I am, once again, in the right place.

The morning air still has touches of sheer coldness as a sherpa starts the wood burning stove. Another brings me a bowl of hot water. I decide to use my water to wash my hair. I know it probably isn't a great idea with my cough, but my hair is awful and I cannot stand it another day. Perspiration has matted my hair so I can barely get a comb through it. Ed comes along and wants to wash his hair, too. We laugh the entire time while standing in freezing temperatures pouring bowls of hot water over each other's head. It is fun, and it feels like another luxury. Little things do take on a whole new meaning. Water is a spiritual symbol. What a hot shower would feel like right now! I think of moments at home when I am in the shower. I visualize the water coming down all over me as White Light. It covers me and goes through me. It embraces and surrounds me with a protective coating. I place a rainbow of Light outside the White Light, because everyone wants to connect with the Light and I may not want them to connect with me in a physical or harmful way. I start each day with the shower Light around and through me, and the rainbow of Light as my shield. I include positive statements, such as "may my words today bring wisdom, joy, connection and caring to others" and these words are being said as I am swallowing water from the shower so my body can take in these words and become part of my wholeness.

The shower experience can be a powerful healing tool. Shortly before leaving for Nepal, I was told by a doctor that I had a 4.5 centimeter sized cyst on my ovary. It was serious and too large to ignore at my age. I had to make a decision. Immediate surgery or wait and see if it grew any larger. I decided to wait. He told me not to wait more than a couple of weeks. Every morning while I was in the shower, I visualized the water turning into a green light and massaging my ovaries. I spent many minutes in the shower every morning for two weeks. The green light was constantly with me as I saw the cyst being gently massaged and embraced in that light. I returned to the doctor two weeks later. He was amazed. The cyst had disappeared. He didn't know how that had happened. I did. I knew I could take my trip to the Himalayas. There was no problem.

After breakfast some of the group want to take another day hike. Ann and I are too tired, and we stay in our sleeping bags in the common room most of the day talking about people and relationships. She told me something very important that was worth learning. She said she and her boyfriend Bill do not blame each other for hurts and misunderstandings toward one another. If something is done that offends one of them, the idea is that that hurt damaged the relationship, and not them personally. The solution was what could the person do to heal the relationship? That philosophy removes them personally from the issue and allows room for correction and healing. It sounds healthy to me. I will try it, someday, if I am ever in a relationship again. One of my biggest problems is taking things too personally. That gets in my way in groups and in relationships. However, I am not sure I will ever be in a significant relationship again, not because I don't want to, but because I don't need to be.

Amy returns early. The guys are still hiking. I don't know how they do it. Ann and Amy decide to walk to Namache Bazaar. It is the biggest village for miles around and there are many shops. I feel up to going with them. I have missed not really getting to know my trekking friends. I wish I could stay up with them on the trail. Even though I have been in my sleeping bag all day, I am fully dressed so I get up and put on my parka so I can go with Ann and Amy.

As we walk down the steps from the lodge into the village, the yaks come through the narrow village streets and everyone has to get out of their way. There is no right of way for us on the road; these guys are bigger and much more sure-footed than any of us. But I am not jumping as fast or as high anymore. I learned that the other day during lunch. The yaks don't want to hurt anyone. They are just moving through life like the rest of us. They are doing the best they can, just as I am. I hear myself saying that a lot lately, *"I am just doing the best I can"*. I only wish the struggles were not as difficult as they seem to be in my life. I suppose pain is relative. There are many who have had a great deal more pain than I will see in many lifetimes. I am not interested in counting the pain trophies I have. I just want to know why I chose to make my life so hard, and how I stop it from being that way? The yaks have moved on, and I wander through the open air shops knowing I have no answers.

Amy and Ann saunter off and I find myself alone again. Is that by accident or do I make it happen that way? I don't know, but I enjoy the time, so it really doesn't matter. My eyes rest on a mandala. The shopkeeper tells me it is a sterling silver necklace that represents the wheel of life. I decide to buy it, but I'm not sure why. It does seem pretty, and it will be a nice connection for me to the Himalayas. I am certain I will carry the memories in my heart and mind. External sources and trinkets don't give me pleasure anymore. It all seems to come from within. There are symbols on the necklace and I am not sure but, it just feels like the necklace is a reflection of my life's story. I am too tired to have it interpreted for me now. It just feels right.

I am beginning to have trouble breathing again and I need to rest. I have only been gone from the lodge for ten minutes, but I must return. My leg muscles are experiencing spasms again and I am in the sleeping bag when the others return. The late hours with the glow from the wood stove and a little rum makes the evening soft, light and comfortable. The candles are lit and the flames are dancing to their own vibration. A sense of harmony within the room and with everyone is here. Wood is being burned in this stove not pine cones, so the heat makes the common room feel warm and cozy.

I show the necklace to Nima and he tells me that it was made in Tibet. It is a very religious piece of jewelry. It symbolically describes one's life through carving of the metal with red and blue stones in a circle of hearts. Perhaps the blue stands for calm and peace, the red for courage and the hearts for the love I have felt in my life. The hearts on the necklace are connecting. That fits my belief system and my life.

We begin our final climb tomorrow. It will be Christmas Eve day and Nima tells us, we will reach the monastery at dusk.

We all turn in early. We have decided to sleep in the common room with our sleeping bags stretched on the wall to wall cushioned ledges which just fit the width of our sleeping bags. I have trouble sleeping and as I begin to doze I am awakened from breathing sounds. Ed tells me the next morning I sounded like I was having a hard time last night. I was, but I make light of it. No reason to worry. I didn't want to say that I felt like I was drowning in my own fluid all night. I kept gasping for air and could barely get it. I was drowning. Really drowning. I am not sure I can climb today, but I won't tell anyone that. Christmas is tomorrow and the Tengboche Monastery and His Holiness, the high Lama, await our arrival.

Nima said today's hike would not be too hard. Everyone is ahead of me again as they head for the museum in Namache. We are starting the trek by visiting the museum first. We also will be able to take pictures of Mt. Everest and see it clearly. Sherap walks ahead of me. My legs are experiencing spasms again. It is too early in the day for this. My walking sticks are barely holding me up. But then I feel the angels and the white silk cord which is tied around my waist. The museum is only a few minutes outside of town, and once I am there, I feel a little better. It is a modern-looking building on flat ground. We stay in the area for over an hour looking at the pictures and artifacts and taking photos of Mt. Everest and our group. Now I am feeling inspired, even if I am weak. I can make it today. I *will* make it. The doubt is diminishing. The Buddhist philosophy says intention is most important. If my intention is clear, then chances are whatever I intend to happen will happen. Throughout this trip it is and has been my intention to meet the Lama and connect with him. Intention is very powerful, and I am feeling the power of it in every step I take.

We are climbing again. Everyone is out of sight and I am using my walking sticks. The phlegm and blood are still a problem, but I don't know how serious right now. I am far too busy concentrating on reaching my goal. My body is shaking and I feel the quivering, especially in my legs. I wonder if they can continue to hold me up? The angels are here. I feel their presence and their power. They, too, want me to meet the Lama on Christmas Day. The river is rushing below us as we cross another swing bridge. It is a very poorly constructed bridge, and seems very unsafe, but it is the only way to get over the river, and so I walk carefully, holding onto the ropes that serve as barriers from the river. The climb continues and the challenge is present.

I ask Sherap for my camera again. These little paper disposable cameras have taken some good pictures for me in the past. I hope the pictures in the Himalayas are good ones. It feels like they will be, and I smile to myself.[5]

We continue to climb as the sun is setting. It is Christmas Eve, and I am beginning to wonder if I will get to the monastery before dark. I an certain I will get there; I just don't know when. Sherap is farther ahead and I am walking alone. I take one step at a time. I am now in this moment and no longer thinking about the next. The **Course in Miracles** words come to my mind.[6]

> *Heaven is here. There is nowhere else.*
> *Heaven is now. There is no other time. M.58*

---

[1]The King James version of the **Holy Bible** (1974)

[2]**I have a Dream** sung by ABBA and written by Swedish composers Anderson and Ulvaeus (Union Songe Musikforlag AB, Sweden music and Polar Music AB).

[3]The picture taken is the front cover of this book. The negative has a high density of light. **Ziba Color Lab's** letter confirms the negative has more light than their equipment could normally match. You may need to expand your frame of reference but if you choose to see her, the angel may appear (See Appendix for letter).

[4]**The Happy Prince** is a children's classic fairy tale.

[5]The picture on the back cover was taken on Christmas Eve Day is called the Circle of Rainbow Light. Months later I learn that the Tengboche Monastery sect is called the Rainbow sect. Synchronicity continues to be present in all that I am.

[6]**The Course in Miracles** was channeled by Helen Schuoman, a professor of medical psychology at Columbia University. It was published by the Foundation for Inner Peace, Tiburon, CA (1975).

CHAPTER FOUR: **HEART TO HEART WITH THE LAMA**

My wool slacks feel very loose; I must be losing weight. But that isn't important right now. Given how weak I feel, I surprise myself when I am able to continue walking and climbing, but somehow I do. Amy comes back to join us, but it is obvious I am slowing her down, so she doesn't stay long.

Every two or three minutes I stop to breathe more deeply so I can fill my weakened lungs with air. When the trail requires it, I climb on hands and knees over the boulders, while at other times I carefully place my feet where Sherap has left his footprints. His footing is sure. Yet he gives me space to walk on my own. He always seems to know what I need next, without my having to ask. He is sensitive, quiet, and aware. Sherap has reassured me this part will be easier, but I still find every step a challenge. Now Sherap has moved a few minutes ahead of me on the trail and I begin to worry that I may have to walk several hours in the dark.

I am placing one foot ahead of the other. That is all I can do. I look down at the ground when it gets difficult. Sometimes my eyes close. I can't help it. Keeping them open seems so difficult. I just don't have the energy to focus. But I am breathing deeply, and with determination.

I am stopping every few steps, trying to fill my stomach with air through deep breathing. I am coughing up a considerable amount of blood and phlegm and I feel weak and dizzy. Heaven may be even closer than I realize. My walking sticks are holding me up and I continue the climb. The villagers walk by, and their smiles turn to looks of concern when they glance back at me. The forest and mountains are serene. Even though my body is not cooperating, I feel centered in this experience and I remain present. Quietness surrounds me, and yet I do not feel alone. The angels are very close, and are still working hard to help me reach my destination. The white satin cord is resting around my waist whenever I stop for a breath. Then it tightens as it pulls me up the mountain. I am exhausted, but I will not give up.

It is becoming dusk and the night chill comes on quickly. I turn the corner. There is Sherap standing in front of a giant boulder and to his right the Tengboche Monastery sits behind him. He smiles and whispers to me, "you are here. You have made it."

It is Christmas Eve. I am here! Tears well up and I stop just where I am. My feet do not want to move. My eyes only want to take in the beauty of the monastery and of Sherap smiling. Sherap and I smile at each other. He welcomes me to one of the most spiritual places on earth. I am in awe of myself and everything around me, and I am grateful. *"Thank you, God, for allowing me to be here," I say silently.* We will walk thirty more minutes to the lodge, but I feel the energy and strength to go on.

We walk quietly and slowly. Neither of us speak. The energy is strong and distinct. It touches every part of my being. The path seems easier now. It is getting dark but Sherap is by my side and it seems the monastery is just a few steps behind me. We arrive at the lodge. It is made out of rock. It is a solid looking structure and I am told a woman's monastery is further down the trail, but I am not able to go that far now.

My resilient spirit has gotten me to the top of the mountain. The struggles have been enormous, but I didn't give up. My gentle, receiving side seems so far out of reach. Did I ever have one or has it been lost because I haven't felt safe for such a long time?

We walk into the lodge and everyone applauds. I think there may have been bets on whether I was going to make it or not. My friends may know at some level how spiritually important it is for me to be here at the monastery on Christmas Day. Amy, Bill and Ann are not doing well. They decide to forego the Christmas Eve gathering of the group. They have the headaches and nausea that accompany altitude sickness, but the medicine my doctor gave me masks my symptoms. I am not suffering from a headache or nausea, just coughing up a lot of blood, but no one knows. I do feel lightheaded. I find my cubicle and place my sleeping bag on the bed. I rest for a while, but I am too excited to stay quiet for long. I want to put on a clean sweater for Christmas Eve, comb my hair, spray on some perfume, and put on make-up for the first time in ten days. I am trying to hide the two very big fever blisters on my mouth. I find some lipstick I didn't know I had and it helps (vanity continues to exist). My thoughts return to a conversation with a friend earlier in the year. "Looking attractive is important to me," I said with a smile. He responded, "Jerri, what about wisdom?" I smiled and said, "Oh, can't wisdom be pretty?" He didn't pursue the conversation. The point was made. For me, it isn't the fear of getting old; just a feeling of joy in reflecting beauty — inside and out.

It is Christmas Eve and I am at the monastery! I am going to celebrate, and I am too excited to rest anymore. Intention is powerful and my intention is being fulfilled. I return to the common room, and I meet two families who are also staying at the lodge. The wood stove is burning brightly. The room is warm and the candles give a peaceful glow. We all decide to sit around the potbelly stove with our feet up on the wood block resting beneath it. We are enjoying the warmth while temperatures outside are below freezing. Ed is also here. Children join us - now it is truly Christmas Eve. It feels good. I love the light and harmony among us. There is an awareness here that I don't feel in other places. This centeredness reflects my higher self in all its richness.

The adults discuss their experiences in the Himalayas. There is a difference here - a feeling that I find comfortable. I don't feel this in most places, but it is here. A sense of intimacy and connection are very much in this room of strangers and I am home.

As we talk, I take out a star candle I brought so that I could observe the Christian tradition of giving gifts on Christmas. I have been told the candle contains crystals and charms and they can be retrieved with tweezers as the candle burns. As I offer it, I notice a story is included. One of the men wants to read it.

Once upon a time in a distant land, there lived a fair princess who was in love with a brave young knight. But alas the knight was imprisoned by a most evil king. After longing for her beloved for many a month, the princess conceived a clever plan. She traveled to a mystical kingdom deep within the earth where she gathered crystals and stones with magical powers. Upon returning home, she made a candle in which she concealed the treasures. Then she arranged to have it delivered to her lover in his cold dark dungeon. The sad and disheartened knight welcomed the gift of light and immediately burned his candle, unaware of its special powers. When the crystal revealed itself, a rainbow appeared from within. A wave of joy and love swept through him as he realized the special nature of the gift. At that moment, the crystal in the candle the princess was burning also shimmered with a rainbow. Then lo and behold, the two tiny rainbows soared out into the heavens and became one. The power of their love was so great that they were drawn into the rainbow's arc where neither prison walls nor evil kings could ever keep them apart. Within each treasure candle, you will find a crystal and other gifts of the earth, each with their own special power. Hold your crystal up to the light. You just might see the beginning of your own magic rainbow. With love and rainbow wishes, the keeper of the flame[1]

After the story is read, I take my tweezers, remove a small crystal, another stone and a charm – which is an Aladdin's lamp – from the candle, and give them as gifts to Ed and the two couples.

Fascinating. More double rainbows appear in my life and isn't it wonderful it is on Christmas Eve at the monastery? Now do I believe in synchronicity? Of course! It is how I live my life. Sherap walks into the room quietly and stays for a brief few minutes and then leaves again. I am sure Sherap would have liked the story if he had arrived earlier. I was surprised to hear about the double rainbows. They seem to be everywhere on this trip. I take the string of gold stars that was wrapped around the candle. That is my gift. I am at the highest of highs and stars are a fitting symbol. Divine Order is in place on this Christmas Eve.

Nima comes in and tells us we will be meeting His Holiness Rinpoche Ngawang Tenzin Jangpo[2] tomorrow. He suggests we purchase white silk scarves so His Holiness may give us his blessings with the scarves. Nima is pleased at being able to arrange our meeting. I am still not surprised. I fully expected this meeting even though I was told to expect the unexpected. I am feeling smug. I know I would not have put myself through the ordeal of the past ten days if connecting with the Lama wasn't going to happen. He is part of this moment in Divine Order and we will finally meet tomorrow. I say nothing, but I am smiling.

Nima leaves and the others continue talking, but I begin to have difficulty following the conversations. I drift in and out. The couples are talking about climbing higher tomorrow, and they have small children. It is a difficult climb for anyone, especially with small children. Incredible strength and stamina! My admiration goes to them. I know I have climbed high enough. I just want to meet the Lama tomorrow on Christmas Day. That will be my highest of highs. I excuse myself and head for bed.

Christmas Eve night is uncomfortable. We are at 12,680 feet above sea level and the altitude makes it difficult for all of us. All night I toss and turn, barely sleeping. I cough into my pillow so I won't wake anyone else. I am still gurgling a lot. I am making gasping and rattling sounds in my lungs. The blood is very heavy and I am running out of tissues. It is so hard to breathe.

On Christmas morning, I hardly touch my breakfast. I know I need to eat more, but I can't. Nima tells the others that we are going to meet the Lama in his private residence later that day. Nima has brought us the long white silk scarves decorated with spiritual symbols. It is a tradition, in Nepal, to bring such scarves to the Lama for his blessing. Later, you can leave the scarf at the altar, as a sign you have left your troubles behind, or you may receive it as a blessing and take it with you.

It is mid-afternoon and we leave the lodge for the monastery. Sherap is not with us, and I am quite aware of this as we walk. It feels strange not to have him here. He has been with me from the beginning. Where is he? I could always feel his energy nearby.

As has been my habit, I stay a little behind the others. I want to be alone. When we arrive at the monastery, they remove their shoes and enter, but I linger on the front steps taking in the surrounding mountains and their beauty.

The monastery is made of wood and stone. It is the largest structure I have seen in the Himalayas. I notice a number of small buildings on the grounds. One of them is the private residence of His Holiness Rinpoche Ngawang Tenzing Jangpo.

When the others leave the sanctuary, I enter. Immediately, I notice the altar, the statue of Buddha seated upon it, and some white silk scarves hanging nearby.

I circle around the wooden columns to the left,[3] and stand at the altar for a minute; then I find a place to sit quietly. The sanctuary is filled with rainbow colors inside, and embellished with gold-leaf. The many reds, blues and yellows painted on the walls and posts brighten up the sanctuary. It has a warmth that immediately welcomes its guests. Buddha sits regally at the altar and candles are burning. White silk scarves are hung over the banisters. The floors and pews are wooden. It is new and yet it feels rustic. The former sanctuary, that had been built hundreds of years earlier, had burned down in 1988. Progress had intervened with a new electrical system and had caused the fire. The six-century-old culture was still present without the original Buddhist hamlet. I wish I could have seen the original sanctuary. It feels to me as if the East and West have come together, in this room, and I feel it internally. I feel I belong here.

I sit in the back pew against the wall and rest my head. I am alone in the sanctuary and alone with my thoughts. I don't know why it is so important to be here, but I know that it is. Why was I so driven? Would a spiritual awakening occur? Would I hear the inner voice? Would there be a sign? Perhaps some symbol or a moment of synchronicity that would make me chuckle and I would be richer for the insight I had gained. Was I here to share something of myself? Was I here to reclaim something I had lost? Was I here just to feel the energy? Perhaps I am *just to be* without knowing why. The questions continue and I stop and allow the silence to fill my being. Breathing deeply, I am able to touch the Light and the Light touches me. Now the silence is beautiful.

My eyes are closed and I begin to meditate. God is speaking to me. I am once again exactly where I belong on Christmas Day. My life has felt so synchronized for the past four years. Divine Order is in my awareness. How fortunate I am to be here.

I think of the Dalai Lama, who said, "Christians believe they have to continue to struggle." There are four truths in understanding pain (**The Buddhism of Tibet**, 1975):

The first truth is the realization there is pain in life.

The second truth is how we respond to the pain.

The third truth is understanding the cause of pain.

The fourth truth is knowing that pain can be released and an end to experiencing pain can occur in one's life.

I know and have learned, in some ways, how to embrace the first three truths of pain, but I haven't yet arrived at the fourth one. Maybe after this trip. Maybe in the coming year. I know I am now in my rightful place, embracing the essence of harmony. The Buddhist philosophy states that through struggle, enlightenment comes. The release of pain comes through compassion, but I have a long way to go. My anger seems to be my biggest stumbling block. Sometimes that anger gets in the way of my experiencing compassion for others, but I am learning. I am not always as spiritual as I would like to be. I am just as human as I am spiritual. The integration of those two is the challenge.

I send blessings to my daughter, and tears come to my eyes with thoughts of our separation. I come to terms with it through meditation. Separation is the hardest lesson in my life.

As I sit quietly, my vision rests on a young, dark haired girl wearing a white dress and a flower in her hair. My daughter is part Native American Indian on her father's side and looks very much like the young girl in my meditation. This girl is not wearing shoes, and she's walking down a dusty road like one in an old western town. As she kicks up the dust with her feet, she realizes there is glass in the dirt. She sits down on a raised wooden sidewalk and begins to cry while picking the glass out of her bleeding feet. A wise old man walks by, and she yells for him to come back and help her. He turns, but he doesn't approach her or kneel down. He asks her to explain her problem. She responds, "I have glass in my feet and they're bleeding. Please help me. Can't you help me?"

The wise old man continues to stand and replies that he feels she has the knowledge and skills to help herself. She is desperately looking around for help, when her eyes rest on his feet. She points to them and says, "What are those?" The man replies, "They are shoes." She says, "give them to me so my feet won't hurt anymore." The man shakes his head. "These are my shoes," he says. "I trust you have the knowledge and skills to create your own pair of shoes," and he turns to walk on. She yells after him, "Aren't you going to help me? Please help me." He stops, turns and pulls a clean and ironed handkerchief from his pocket, and tells her, "This is a clean and ironed handkerchief that you may use temporarily. Please have it washed, ironed and folded and leave it here tomorrow. I will pick it up on my daily walk, for you see there will be others who will come after you, who will also need the use of this cloth. I trust you will return it as it is now." The man then continues his walk.

A feeling of loving detachment will help me in this ultimate experience of separation. I also know my daughter must come into her own experience of the Light. We each have that right, and I honor her in her journey.

Spiritual consciousness allows me to enter into a dialogue with the sacred Presence that is in the sanctuary. I feel myself being welcomed and received. The Buddha's arms open to embrace me.

Then I rise, and as I turn to the right to return to the sanctuary doors, I come full circle in the sanctuary, and perhaps, in my life. I don't want to leave this special place. That's what I am thinking when I hear Nima tell us we are now going to meet His Holiness, the Lama, in his private residence.

We walk a short path to his house and enter. His Holiness Rinpoche Ngawang Tenzing Jangpo greets each of us at the door with a bow. He is a small fair-skinned man with a clean-shaven head. His eyes are crystal clear. He is fully present. I always know when someone meditates a lot. The energy is completely present in the body and the eyes are focused and steady. His Holiness reflects these qualities as we are introduced. I immediately feel comfortable in his presence. It's as if our souls are already acquainted.

"My Light is honored to meet your Light," I say softly. "It is my hope our Lights can join in the wholeness." I knew for months that this is how I would greet him, because

I had known for months we would meet.

He nods and smiles. Nima translates briefly, and the Lama appears to understand and he smiles with his eyes.

One by one, we stand before the Lama as he places the silk scarves around our shoulders and blesses us in Nepalese. Then he invites us to sit down, and I find myself sitting to his immediate right. Amy sits alongside me. The others sit to Amy's right.

The Lama explains the spiritual symbols on the scarves and Nima translates. The entire time, I am conscious of reining my energy in, rather than allowing it to take over the room. I want very much for everyone to feel space for their own Light to expand. I am very aware of honoring the space of others. I need to give others around me their own space. I haven't been very good at that in the past. I don't know if I have even been conscious of it until now. I hope I can learn that this year, too. Why am I so conscious of that limitation right now? I don't know, but it pervades my thoughts.

I want so much to ask the Lama question after question, but I limit myself to two, so others will have a chance. I ask Nima for permission to ask my first question. He nods. This is why I have come to the Himalayas. I am not aware of the question, but it begins to surface as the memory of all the difficult moments in my life flood through me. My eyes begin to mist over. The words catch in my throat, but slowly they come.

"The first half of my life has been very hard," I begin. "What do I need to do so that the second half will be..." I cannot think of the word. I begin to weep as tears fall down my cheeks.

Amy leans toward me and whispers: "Easy?"

"Yes, easy..." What I am thinking is, I hope the American men can't see me crying. My feminine vulnerability is coming through loud and clear. I am not used to showing this so publicly. My aloofness has been my trademark. My friends have told me that often. My dominant masculine energy got me here, and now my feminine energy is taking over and expressing in a way that surprises even me.

Even as I think this, I notice the concern in the Lama's eyes. He leans toward me as he gently speaks:

"Treat everyone and everything the same."

He repeats this several times, while Nima translates.

I take a deep breath, taking in His Holiness' words, and the meaning behind them.

There is silence among us. The depth of the response will take time to internalize and embrace. No one says anything for quite a while. Eventually it appears that no one is planning to ask a question, so I regain my composure and ask a second: "What is your holiest holiday and how do you celebrate it?" He tells us about Mani Rimdu, a three-day festival that takes place in the Solu Khumbu region where the monastery is located. His face lights up as he tells us about the celebration. The question appears to make him happy. He tells us that people come from everywhere. It is a sherpa holiday. They set up tents, and the food preparations are elaborate. The intention is to come together from far distances to experience great joy.

I wish we could talk for hours, even days. I wish he could teach me about Buddhism. I wish I could know more about him. I wish I could know about everything that surrounds us in this holy place. But I do not ask another question. I need to practice giving space to others. However, I also am not sure I need to ask any

more questions. I feel I have come for the answer to the question I have asked. Now I feel complete.

I present my gift to His Holiness. It is to celebrate my holy holiday. It is a white, globe-shaped candle that has the world continents on it in gold overlay. There are stars around the clear plastic covering the globe. I give the Lama the candle and he says he will have one of his monks place it on the altar in the sanctuary. I am forgetting my

117

feelings of sickness. I am so glad I am here. Meeting the Lama was more than I desired it to be. What a wise person and truly gentle man. His gift to me is significant. It is a most important lesson for me to learn. We honor one another with a bow, and then say good-bye with our eyes.

I feel a tremendous amount of peace, and these feelings are going through me and around me. I think of the driver on the highway who cuts me off, and then I see myself holding a beautiful infant in my arms. Every experience I have - treat it the same. How is that done? It will take a long time to ponder and probably years to practice successfully. It is my vow to begin practicing the Lama's lesson immediately. I have no doubt I will slip many times, but my intention is pure. His lesson is not about letting others take advantage of me. If I can remain calm within my heart, no matter what the external experiences, then my response will be the same toward everyone. Honoring my integrity and remaining centered will allow me to express my power without violating the space of those around me. It will take work, but I am willing.

We return to the santurary steps. The monks have been given the globe candle. They are delighted with the little gold stars; part of the wrapping. They are standing on the top steps after placing the candle on the altar. I watch them play with the stars. They appear so curious about the shiny, sparkling, little gold objects. Their playfulness is contagious. They are adult young men but they are like children with a new toy. I have my stars from the star candle and the monks have their stars from the globe candle. We are sharing the stars. This feels like heaven. I smile even more.

I decide to go back in the sanctuary and I see Nima as he honors the Buddha in a prostrate position. His face rests against his hands on the wooden floor and his legs lay side by side. A quiet and humble human being is honoring the religion he knows through deep meditation. I leave quietly so as not to disturb him, and put my shoes back on again. The Buddhists seem to live their spirituality. Everything I have seen this week convinces me of their sincerity and commitment to family and service. Sherap comes from around the corner near the Lama's home. I feel his energy once again. He has been with His Holiness. I know that without being told. Sherap smiles at me and walks back to the lodge on his own.

Although the Americans are lingering at the entrance of the sanctuary, I decide to start walking down the stairs. As I reach the bottom step of this very long staircase, I turn to the right, and see the Lama twenty feet away. He sees me, and we greet one another with a gentle wave and smiling eyes. Eyes, of course, are the window to the soul.

We smile at each other, and in that smile is the knowledge that something sacred has passed between us. The intimacy in sharing our spirituality is significant. I am with the highest of highs. The mountain shares her power and presence with me just as I choose to share mine.

It is a truly sweet moment. I feel recognized for who I am.

---

[1]**Treasure Candle, Ltd.** has given permission to reprint the Fable of the Treasure Candle. These candles can be ordered through Treasure Candle, Ltd., in No. Hollywood, California.

[2]After learning that His Holiness Rinpoche Ngawang Tenzing Jangpo is the highest ranking Lama in Nepal, I find out the Tengboche Monastery is considered one of the most sacred in Nepal. I was with the highest of highs near the highest of highs (Mt. Everest) on Christmas Day!

[3]Many months later, I learned that upon entering a Buddhist sanctuary, it is proper to walk clockwise. I had not been in one before Tengboche but unconsciously I knew how to approach the altar; not straight on, but in a circle.

 CHAPTER FIVE: **SURRENDER**

In my quiet journey from the monastery back to the lodge, many thoughts come into my awareness. I have received my answer, and until connecting with the Lama, I had not consciously realized how important that question was to me. Perhaps losing my passport and traveler's checks brought me to the realization of just how hard my life has been, and put me in touch with such a personal question. I could not help but shake my head though. Why was I so worried that the American men might see me cry? Was I that far from trusting men?

Strange, I feel connected to the Nepalese men. Sherap and I have a bond that will exist throughout our lives. It was my intention to meet the Lama at the monastery on Christmas Day. Months ago when my intention was just a thought, I didn't know how important that thought would become. It took on a life of its own. With one step at a time I reached my destination, and I received my answer. I received much more than that, really. I felt recognized for who I really am. Maybe the men from my past never gave me that experience and maybe I never gave any of them that gift either. I am indebted to His Holiness, and I will hold his wisdom and gentleness close to my heart.

I am returning to the sherpa lodge for an overnight stay, and then we are to climb back down the mountain for the next week. I have gotten to the top of the mountain; will I be able to get back down? I have reached many mountain tops in my life. What will my return experience be? I don't know if I can make the return trip. I will try. Majestic Mt. Everest stands nearby and it is more beautiful than anything I could have imagined. I am connecting with the highest of highs and it is great!

I received my answer and maybe there are more along the way. I am open to the experience. I wish I had been able to spend time with the other sherpas on this trip. They each have a shyness that is unique. They look down when I talk to them, and they do it with a subtle smile. I know they like me. We have smiled at each other from a distance throughout the trip. They are very hard-working people. All of them, except for Sherap, wear torn and dirty slacks and shirts. A few have scarves and gloves. Most of the time I see them in wool shirts but seldom in heavy jackets. I don't know how they get along in such freezing temperatures.

Nima, our head guide, stayed at the lead with the Americans climbing the fastest. The other three sherpas were somewhere in the middle. They carried our duffle bags, three at a time, weighing 30 pounds each. Ninety pounds on a one hundred and forty pound body climbing up a mountain of rocks and crossing swing bridges made of ropes is an amazing accomplishment. These men have been born and brought up in the mountains, but their strength is more than a familiarity with the terrain. None of them speak English except Nima and Sherap. I learn that one of the sherpas is fifteen years old. The other two are in their twenties. Nima appears to be in his early forties. They are a very close knit group, and seem to have a lot to talk about when they are together.

At night when I walk past the kitchen, I see the sherpas sitting around the stove, talking and laughing together. There has been no fighting or disagreements between any of them throughout the trip. They respect Nima and Sherap a great deal. It can be seen in their manner even though I don't understand what is being said. They also have a respectful attitude toward one another as co-workers. Mt. Everest is an extremely remote wilderness area. They have to depend on each other during these climbs. There are no telephones. No radios. No doctors. All they have is each other and they know it.

I don't know the other sherpas, but I do know Sherap. He is a very kind person and his friends appear to be, too. The path to the Tengboche Monastery was easy. It is Christmas Day. It feels like I spent a lifetime getting here, and it was worth it. Sherap must have gone ahead; he isn't anywhere to be found. Nima joins me on the walk back to the sherpa lodge.

I am laughing as Nima talks. Sometimes tears come to my eyes as he shares parts of his life with me. He talks about his divorce and the pain it caused him. He talks about his children and his new wife, whom he loves very much. He is so open with me. I wonder if it is because he saw my vulnerability and openness with the Lama? Does he feel safe with me? Has he seen the real, and feminine Jerri, and does he like her? It seems that way.

He is smiling a lot and his eyes are twinkling as we walk along the path. I like this man. He is shorter than I am and he must weigh about what I do. He probably weighs 135 pounds. He has a small frame, but appears to have a strength that, at first glance, is not obvious to the eye. He is showing his vulnerability, but I have no doubt that he is strong physically, and probably emotionally too. It confirms my belief that true strength is connected to vulnerability. I know the more vulnerable I am, the stronger I am. If I hide that vulnerability, it is because I am afraid I will be rejected or ridiculed. The tough overcoat of anger and aggressiveness I have worn on many occasions just hides the vulnerability Nima saw in me earlier. In my past I haven't allowed many men to see that - maybe that will change? What a nice validation. Nima is being real with me now.

Nima and I discuss our past issues of anger. It is an emotion I need to outgrow. I will have it until I realize it no longer serves any useful purpose, and it inhibits my development. It closes doors to the human heart, as my automatic writing told me years earlier. I don't want to stuff the anger when I feel it; I just need to express it without letting anyone or anything be its target. I need to scream and yell in my car as I am driving alone, so no one will have to listen to me. I will need to hit a punching bag when I am feeling anger. I will need to write more about my feelings in my journal. I am certainly not going to let it eat me up inside; that might cause cancer and heart attacks. Over the past year, I have released a great deal of anger, but more has built up over recent events in my life. Upon returning home, and with time, I hope to release the anger that I have recently been carrying. There is no room in my heart for it any longer.

Right now I am thoroughly enjoying my conversation with Nima. I won't tell him how sick I am feeling. I'll be fine. I fulfilled my intention. I met the Lama on Christmas Day at the monastery and Mt. Everest is very near. I am at the highest of highs and it is more than I alone could have created. This is, indeed, heaven.

Night is falling fast. The chill in the air is feeling worse than any of the other nights. Perhaps it is because we are so much closer to Mt. Everest, or maybe because my resistance is weakening. I continue to have trouble breathing, and the phlegm is greener than ever, and the bleeding excessive. I know I am good at hiding my illness because image is important to me. Few have seen my vulnerable side. I haven't wanted to let anyone know how vulnerable I have felt on this trip. I also didn't want them to make me go back down the mountain before meeting the Lama. Nothing was more important to me than that. Nothing. The angels knew it. The Universal Presence pulling the white satin cord on the other end knew it. Nothing was going to stop me and I am glad nothing did. It was worth everything! I wouldn't advise anyone else to do what I have done, but I am glad I have had this experience.

We are back at the lodge and it seems pretty quiet. Bill, Ann, Amy and Ed arrive as Nima and I are finishing our conversation. Nima said he is going to start preparing dinner and he will call us when it is ready. I ask Nima if we are going back down the mountain tomorrow the same way we came up, and he says yes. I was hoping there was a super highway on the other side of the mountain with a bus that could take me back. Everyone laughs. No, Nima, says. No super highway. We will go back the same way we came up. I express my vulnerability in the only way I know how. Maybe I should call some of my friends in California and have them send a helicopter for me. Everyone laughs again and they roll their eyes. Oh, come on Jerri. No helicopters around here.

I nod and slowly say, "I know." For right now, I just need to rest, and I go to my cubicle. I will think about tomorrow tomorrow. Where have I heard that before? The thirty-minute walk from the monastery went fast with Nima's company, but it was still strenuous and my walking sticks came in handy again. I don't know what I would have done without them on the trek.

I am going to rest for a while. Amy knocks at my door telling me dinner is ready, but I can't seem to get up. I tell her to go on without me. I didn't think I would be eating dinner and I just want to sleep. There is a couple with two small children in the cubicle next to mine. Bill and Ann are down the corridor, and Amy is right across from me. I don't know where Ed's cubicle is, but we are all on the same floor, so he is somewhere in the area. I need to go to the bathroom before it gets too dark. The potty bucket is not the easiest thing to use, but then the outhouse can be worse. Just a small wooden shack with a hole in the floor and wooden slats on either side of the hole. The waste falls down the mountain directly in to the river. We were told earlier not to drink from the river because it is contaminated from villages upstream and from lodge outhouses such as ours. There is no indoor plumbing. In most of the places there is no electricity. There are no radios, not even portable ones. No need for them because there aren't any radio stations, anyway.

I opt for the potty bucket. I am not sure I can walk down the six steps and a hundred feet to the outhouse. I can't seem to stay warm even in my wool slacks, sweater, wool Pjs, gloves and hat and in the sleeping bag with a thermal blanket over me. There is too much blood coming up. I feel very alone, even though I can hear the people downstairs in the common room. It is Christmas night and they seem to be celebrating. A number of people who are staying at the lodge are climbing on their own. They are not part of our group, and they sound like they may be from Germany. The wood slats in the floor are thin and there is a lot of space between the slats. Several of the people are smoking downstairs, and the smoke is rising through the floor. I can hardly breathe, and my weak lungs are trying to fight off the cigarette smoke. The cubicles are not very private. The walls only go to about six feet in height, so I can talk to the lady next door. She is upset about the smoke, too. Her name is Terry, and she decides to go downstairs and tell the trekkers to move away from our area. I hope it helps. I am not able to get out of bed to go with her. I would if I could; I just can't get up.

The smoke seems less now, but the conversations go on for hours. It doesn't make any real difference. I am not able to sleep anyway. I am not even sure that I would wake up if I fell asleep. I am coughing up too much phlegm and blood, and my lungs are making that gurgling, drowning sound. I can hear Terry talking to a man in the corridor. She is telling him about me. She has heard me coughing and said it doesn't sound good. It has been decided I may have pneumonia or at least a very bad cold. I don't have a headache or nausea, so altitude sickness is ruled out.

The man is a doctor. I don't invite him into my cubicle. I tell him I will be alright. I am going home tomorrow. I don't tell them I have been coughing up blood for four days. I am not thinking rationally. I cannot make a decision. I just know I can't get out of this bed right now.

It is Sunday morning and I hear Amy and the others packing for our trip back down the mountain. I won't make it. I can't even get dressed. I just won't make it. I pull myself out of the bed and walk the few feet to Ann and Bill's cubicle. I ask if I can talk to Bill alone. I don't want to make a scene and I feel more comfortable talking to just one person rather than several. Bill walks back to my cubicle with me. He sees the tissue with blood. There is a lot of blood. I tell him I won't make it down the mountain. I just won't make it. He looks stunned. He and the others didn't realize how bad it was. Now he knows. He wants me to go downstairs with him to talk to Nima. I can't walk down the steps. He will be right back. He will bring Nima with him.

Nima and Bill are standing over my bed. Nima tells me, "Sherap just left. He is running to Namache. It usually takes seven hours one way, but I know Sherap and he will make the trip very fast. He will try to get a helicopter in here for you today. Don't worry. The group will follow Sherap and reach Namache this afternoon. We will get someone in here for you. I will have one of my boys stay outside, and if you need anything, let him know. They will give you hot garlic soup and hot tea. If you need help to the outhouse, there is another woman staying here who can assist you. They will keep a close eye on you. For now, stay in bed and we will bring help. Don't worry. Sherap is very worried about you. We all are." We bow our heads toward one another and they leave my cubicle and finish their packing to return to Namache.

Amy and Ann come by my cubicle and ask if they can pack for me. I appreciate what they are doing. They are putting all of my things in the duffle bag. I tell Amy she can have the apple cider packets and turkey jerky, two treats that we have savored on this trip. We hug and I wish them a safe journey down the mountain. I keep apologizing and I don't know why. I feel stupid. Feeling vulnerable does that to me. I just don't like having people see me this way. I don't like being this way. Where is that independent, self-sufficient, initiating and aggressive woman who began this trip in San Francisco, went through Korea and Bangkok, and climbed the mountain to be with the Lama? A very different person seems to be emerging. The thought crosses my mind - I wonder if I will live long enough to see who this new person is?

I hear the Americans leaving. I hope they enjoy the trek down the mountain. I wish I were strong enough to be with them. It's much later and the sherpa brings me hot garlic soup and some lemon tea. It taste good. Mostly water and garlic cloves. That's fine. I can't eat anything solid. I don't have the strength to chew and swallow. The lady is knocking on my door. Do I need to go to the outhouse? Yes. Maybe she can help me. I am leaning on her as she tries to get me down the six steps of the lodge. I am out of breath and don't know if I can walk to the outhouse, but I have gotten this far so I will make it. I won't walk to the outhouse again. It takes too much energy. It is too difficult right now. The inhouse potty bucket is looking better all the time. She is an elderly woman and I don't want to lean too hard on her but I can't stand up by myself. I feel very dizzy and I am not thinking clearly or at all. The remaining sherpa helps me. I don't know what I am saying. I just keep apologizing all the time.

They help me get back to my cubicle and into bed. I am not going to leave my bed again today. It is getting late in the day when the knock comes. It is Sherap's voice! He comes into my cubicle and I start to cry. Sherap! How did you get here so fast?

He is out of breath. He looks dusty and dirty. He ran all the way to Namache and back in ten hours! It is a seven hour trek one way. How did he do that? No need to worry. He is doing alright. He doesn't have good news, though. He couldn't get the helicopter. Nima is negotiating with the pilot now, and Nima will be back tonight to tell me what is being done to get me down the mountain. Sherap wants to know how I am doing. I feel much better seeing him. I will be alright, I think. I am still coughing up a lot of blood. I have trouble standing. Sherap tells me he will be near me. He won't be far away again. If I need anything, just call out. He will hear me. He bows to me and I return the blessing. I am so glad Sherap is here!

It is late, approaching midnight. Nima has returned from Namache, and from the other side of the door he is asking me if I am awake. I ask him to come in. Nima tells me I have two choices. My American friends have a total of $1500 cash, and the helicopter pilot demands $1500 cash (no credit cards or checks). My friends will spend all of their money to get me out by helicopter. My second choice is to have the sherpas fix a straw basket and strap it to the back of a sherpa, and they will take turns carrying me over the mountain for five hours to the evacuation plane in Shyangboche. The sherpas would then rejoin the Americans in Namache, and guide them back down the mountain for the next five days. Either way, I cannot get out until morning. There is no choice. I will not make my American friends sacrifice all of their money for me. They need that money to get back down the mountain. I don't know how these men will carry me, but if they say they can, then I am willing to try it, too.

Nima nods and tells me, "we will leave at 5:15 a.m. We must get to the plane by 10 a.m." I try to sleep, but it's impossible. At 5 a.m. I hear the sherpas talking downstairs. I take off my pjs and struggle putting on two heavy sweaters, my wool slacks, socks and boots. I am grateful that Ann and Amy packed for me yesterday. There is no electricity and my cubicle is very dark. I hope I get everything. Nima knocks on my door and picks up my duffle bag. Sherap gets my backpack and he helps me down the steps.

The sherpas are putting wood slats in the bottom of the basket and a small blanket on top of the slats. They have woven a cloth strap through the basket and are trying to make sure it is balanced. Nima asks me to sit in the basket. There are two cloth foot stirrups hanging in which he places my heels. There is also a horizontal stick on each side of the basket so I can hold on. Part of the basket is cut out so I can sit in it. I am to hold on to the sticks and lean backwards. They act like they have done this before, and I ask if they have. Nima smiles, and says no with a laugh.

Another sherpa is present whom I had not seen before. Nima has hired him for this special trip. One sherpa was needed to stay with the Americans, and he felt they needed five to get me to the airplane. He calls this sherpa, "Boy". He is going to carry me first.

Nima ties the cloth belt around the sherpa's forehead. I am laying in the basket back to back with the slight young man. It doesn't feel balanced and they have me get up for a moment. Sherap holds me while I am standing. Nima adjusts the slats at the bottom of the basket and then he replaces the blanket over the slats. He pulls the cloth belt through another woven area of the straw basket, and now I am to lay in the basket again. Sherap guides me and with the help of the other sherpas, "Boy" begins to stand. I am laying on my back against the back of the sherpa. He is bent over. We are balanced, ready and we begin the journey.

The morning is still dark and it is so quiet. I have not experienced this much quietness before. I can barely see anyone's face in the dark, but I know they are nearby. Nima and Sherap walk behind the basket so they can catch me if we fall. The only sound I hear is the heavy, shuffling feet of the boy. His burden seems tremendous. I am a burden to these men, and they don't seem to mind. Then a thought crosses my mind. These are very spiritual men. They are beautiful men. I am more vulnerable than I have ever been in my life. My feelings of vulnerability are surfacing over and over again on this trip. I now have met men who do not betray that vulnerability. This is a new experience for me. Is it possible to be vulnerable and not have a man betray me?

My eyes are closed and I am thinking back on my moments of betrayal. My moments of pain. My moments near death before. I am near death now. I know that. These men know that. Other men of my life have seen me in vulnerable moments, and most of them betrayed me in those moments. Whether it was abuse or misuse by the men, I gave so many pieces of myself away and most of them expected me to continue doing it. After years of telling my friends I had been sexually harassed one very close friend who knew all the details told me, "Jerri, you were not sexually harassed. You were raped by one man and sexually assaulted by the other." I cried when she said that to me. I kept crying because she was right. I couldn't stop crying. My minister told me, "Jerri, you were physically, emotionally and spiritually battered by several men in your life." That, too, was true, and my tears didn't stop then, either. Perhaps now the crying can stop. The sun is rising and I am beginning to see the sherpas' faces clearly. The Light in their eyes is unmistakable. Nima and Sherap, my safety net, are walking directly behind me. Oh! The basket jerks and suddenly falls toward the edge of the trail. It is a steep ravine area. I can see over the edge and there appears to be no bottom to the canyon. Sherap and Nima grab me as I begin to fall, and catch me in time. The sherpa is on his knees. Is the weight too much to carry? The strain must be terrible. What happened? We are all sitting on the ground catching our breath. The sherpa is alright and I am safe. The wood slat in the bottom of the basket broke and threw us off balance. Nima fixes the slat by wrapping more cloth bands around the wood and puts them under the blanket at the bottom of the basket. Nima will take over now. Every fifteen minutes a sherpa will take the basket and me. None of them can carry the basket longer. They are breathing hard and their feet sound heavy.

We begin the climb again. My eyes mist over as I lay in this basket. I am seeing these beautiful men and their looks of concern for me in one of the most vulnerable moments of my life. These men are very different from the men of my past. Are there more men in the world like these men? There must be, but I had not believed that until now. I know how sick I am. I am not sure I am going to live. I can tell the sherpas don't know either. Some moments I am conscious while in others, I seem to black out. They see all the blood coming up. I keep moving in and out of consciousness. Nima tells the others we have to go faster.

The coldness is excruciating. I am not moving, so I have no body heat. I don't know what my temperature is right now and all I know is I am beginning to shake a lot. I have to will myself to stop. These men have enough to worry about without my moving in this basket. I must remain as still as I possibly can. I have to stop shaking. I, manage, somehow, to will myself to stop shaking. I won't make it any more difficult for my friends.

Villagers are passing us on the trail. They have never seen this before. They stop and look confused. They ask Sherap. He talks to them as we keep moving as fast as we can. Their looks of confusion turn to concern. Sherap has told them I am very ill, perhaps dying, and they must get me to the plane.

The sherpas are giving me everything they have to give. Their masculinity is so beautiful and so courageous. In contrast, I am feeling my femininity. I thought I had lost it so many years ago. Now I am receptive and open, trusting and accepting. I am far more vulnerable than I ever thought possible, and these men are not betraying my openness. They are completely with me. They are present emotionally, physically, and spiritually. I see their faces. There are tears in Sherap's eyes. They are trying to save my life. I am learning there are at least five men in this world who are safe and trustworthy. Perhaps there are more somewhere. I haven't looked for years. I gave up believing this type of man existed. Now I know they do. The sherpas hearts are open and these men are helping me surrender. It is a sweet surrender.

Nima is out of breath. It is very hard for him after having carried me the last time. I see it in his face. The air is so thin up here. We have to stop at a wayside inn for lemon tea and attempt to regain some of their strength. I see the sherpas standing off to the side huddled in deep conversation. It appears to be a serious conversation.

Sherap brings me some hot lemon tea and he sits on the ground beside me as I drink it. I am still in the basket. He asks me if I think I can walk for a few minutes. He seems reluctant to ask me. He tells me the men want to stay and have more tea. I am in such a daze, I don't realize how strange that request is, but in the moment, I say yes, I can walk with Sherap. He helps me up and I lean on him. We take a few steps and walk around the corner. Oh! there is a swing bridge directly in front of us. Sherap asks me if I can walk with him holding me. I tell him yes I will do that. We begin taking one step at a time. Sherap is holding me firmly. I try to hold the rope railing and take one step at a time. I watch our feet, one placed in front of the other, as we attempt to cross the bridge. The river is roaring below us.

The bridge is fragile. As fragile as me? It is a narrow, vulnerable bridge over the raging river below. Step by step, we move slowly across the bridge, inching our way over the wooden slats. Some of them are broken while others feel strong.

Once again I am crossing a stream which reminds me of my melody. We have been pushing through the darkness, mile after mile. Our destination will make it worth the while. I do believe in angels and I am with one at this moment, as we slowly cross the bridge. We have made it to the other side. Sherap tells me to sit down and rest. I tell him I want to continue. Will he hold my hand? He smiles, takes my hand in his and we walk a few steps. East and West meet and we share the moment. The connection is profound. We both feel the spiritual energy when our hands touch. He knows I cannot walk any further, but I am finding strength in his hand. He is sharing with me. I feel his strength and he senses my weakness even though my will is present. He positions me gently on a nearby flat rock, "We will wait for the sherpas; you see, here they come," Sherap tells me.

I look back and see the other sherpas running toward us. Oh, they weren't going to drink more tea! They just didn't know how to get me across the bridge. They could not carry me in that basket across this rope-drawn rickety bridge. We would have all fallen into the gorge. They wanted to protect my dignity, so they had Sherap cover the truth slightly. They are beautiful men, and I love them and they obviously love me.

They place me back in the basket and the six of us continue our journey. It is full daylight now and villagers pass us on the trail. They are sympathetic and their eyes show concern. I wonder quietly if Americans will ever understand and respect connection the way the Nepalese people do? Will Westerners ever get to that place? There are so many disasters going on with earthquakes, fires, and floods; maybe soon we will begin to understand, above all else, the importance of connection with one another. These people know that so perfectly. They reflect it in their attitudes and actions. It shows in their eyes those windows to the soul.

We continue to go through villages and past children walking to their school. It has been hours, and the sherpas are showing tremendous strain in their bodies and breathing. I am not as cold now, but I am still coughing up blood. I continue to sit as still as I possibly can. I don't want to cause any more trouble to these men who are so present with me. There are always one or two directly behind me waiting to catch me or help me if I need it. Sherap smiles at me often. I see love in his eyes along with the constant concern he has shown me on this journey. It is getting late. We need to be at the plane by 10 a.m. or the plane will leave without me.

I ask Nima, "How much further. How much longer?"

Nima tells me, "Oh just a couple of minutes. Right around the corner, Jerri. We are almost there."

"Please let me walk, Nima. I don't want anyone else to see me like this. Please," I ask him.

"No, no, you must not walk. We will carry you," Nima is shaking his head at me.

"Please, Nima. Please. Let me try."

Nima tells the sherpa to stop, and I am now in the basket on the ground. Nima and one of the sherpas help me out of the basket and I begin to stand. Nima is holding my right arm tightly. The other sherpa is holding my left arm tightly. We begin to walk as they hold me steady.

We walk around the bend and a plane is perched on the runway. People rush toward us. A woman comes close and asks me if I am all right. I nod, and the sherpas let go of my arms. The feeling when the sherpas *disconnect* is profound. I notice it immediately as I take a step forward. Everything becomes dark. I am falling to the ground. I can't stop falling. Someone carries me. I can feel myself being strapped into the plane seat. Someone has placed an oxygen mask on my face, and I can feel the air bringing me back to consciousness. I am hearing a voice. "I am a doctor. Can you hear me? I am a doctor. Can you hear me?" The oxygen is coming into my lungs and my brain, and I open my eyes. A man is standing very close. He tells me again that he is a doctor and begins to take my pulse. Can I understand him? I nod. He is talking, but I don't really understand him. I keep fading in and out.

I am trying to talk through the mask. "I need the sherpas' names. I need their names. Please give me their names," I am begging the doctor. I open my eyes. There are many people standing around the plane. "Please get me their names. I have to have their names," I plead with him. I see Sherap standing farther away. He approaches me and hands me a piece of paper with his name and address. We take each other's hands and clasp them together near our hearts. We are very close and the souls of our eyes are touching. There are tears. The love is felt. We bow with our heads. We will see each other again. It is a silent promise. The doctor passes around a piece of paper for all of the sherpas to write their names. Nima comes to me and we clasp hands and the souls of our eyes touch for a moment. We smile at each other. I tell him, "Thank you for saving my life. Thank you, dear friend." Sherap and Nima have tears in their eyes. Oh, God, separation is the hardest lesson in life. Each sherpa approaches me and we clasp hands and the souls of our eyes touch gently in our good-byes.

These men have done much more than save my life. They have given me a whole new life. I can go home and I can see men differently now. I think I might even meet some I can trust. What a gift these men have given me. My God, what a gift! It took five strong and beautiful men to teach me this lesson but teach is what they have done. The angels have blessed me by bringing me on this trip to be with these men. The angels have been on this path. Some have not been seen and others have. These five who have carried me are angels and their efforts have been felt and appreciated. My heart is full.

The doctor returns to my side. He has stopped talking. He looks at me with respect. He shares the Buddhist bow with me. I return the bow with my head bent, my eyes closed and my hands clasped together. He has seen the sweetness that has passed between the sherpas and me. He knows the significance of our connection and now this separation. He has stopped the questions; he knows there are no more questions to ask. He smiles and tells me there will be airport officials in Kathmandu awaiting my arrival.

I am to keep the oxygen mask on the entire flight back to Kathmandu. I nod. It is the first time I feel I have really breathed in a week. The airplane door closes and the pilot positions us on the runway as we begin to take off.

I glance out the window but I do not see the sherpas. Of course, they would not be standing and waiting. They understand commitment. They have fulfilled their commitment to me and much more. The sherpas understand relationship. They have saved my life and they know I am in good hands. Now their responsibility is to my four American friends and they are on their way to be with them. These people do understand and respect people and relationships. I could learn so much from them; I already have. I have surrendered and have received, in return, a whole new world.

The plane arrives in Kathmandu and I am breathing a little better. There are men with a wheelchair waiting for me. The pilot asks if I want to walk or be taken to the terminal in the chair. One of the men on the ground tells the pilot that the doctor called and insisted I be taken by wheelchair. I am not to walk anywhere. Two men help me off the plane and into the chair. There are four men accompanying me to the airport terminal. One speaks English and he tells me J.P., the head sherpa guide, is on his way to the airport. He was called a short time ago. It is the first word he has received about me.

Two porters stand by my wheelchair waiting for J.P. Because I know the only way these men make money is by helping passengers with baggage, I give them each a United States dollar as a tip. One smiles and starts showing it off to the other porters standing around. One United States dollar is highly valued in Nepal. It is a lot of money. That man returns to the terminal for more business. The other refuses to leave my side. Yes, he knows I have tipped him and he is free to go, but he wants to make sure

I am safe and with my driver. He waits longer. He will not leave my side. Everything talks to me. The symbolism in that is fascinating! He will not exploit me, and he will not leave me, and he is expecting nothing else. I have already given him a huge tip. Much more than most of them make in a week. J.P. and a driver come up in their van. The porter gently helps me out of the wheelchair and leads me toward the van. He says he will not leave until I am safely in my car with my driver. As J.P. puts my bags in the van, I hand the porter another dollar bill. At first he refuses, but I insist. I thank him for helping me and staying behind. He bows. He, too, is a practicing Buddhist. The Light shines in his eyes. We say good-bye with a respect that I can now recognize in a man. I just learned it this morning. But I know what the lesson is now. I won't forget it. My judgment in men won't be wrong, even though I may need to practice a bit at first. I will never be exploited or misused by a man again. I can see and feel the difference. How simple! If the Light is in his eyes I will see it, know it and feel it in the deepest part of my being. I never consciously looked for that Light before. Now I won't miss it. The men today have taught me, and I now know the difference. I wonder why I never looked for that Light before in a man? I will from now on; that is my promise to myself.

# CHAPTER SIX: **HOME, WHOLE - A NEW LIFE EMERGES**

J.P. is asking me what happened. I don't know. I think I have pneumonia. I have been very sick, coughing up blood and passing out. He wants to know what I want to do. Should we go to a medical clinic right now? All I want to do is be in bed. Santi will take care of me, J.P. says. She will make sure I have hot garlic soup and hot lemon tea. We drive to the sherpa lodge.

They help me upstairs and into bed. I am so exhausted I just want to sleep but I can't. I am still coughing up phlegm and blood. I'm unable to make decisions. Santi insists I go to a medical clinic right away.

As Santi and her father drive me to the medical clinic, they exchange looks of concern. I am aware they are very quiet, but they keep looking at me and then at each other. The medical clinic isn't too far away. The nurse takes me in to the examination room where I wait for the doctor. She smiles as she walks through the door. She introduces herself and begins asking questions and taking notes. I am still coughing up blood and she sees it. She stops me, saying, "The others will want to hear this one. Wait a minute." She leaves the room and I feel faint and I can no longer sit up straight. I was sitting on the examination table but I can't any more so I curl up in a ball. Three doctors come in to the room. Dr. David is the director of the clinic. Another David comes into my life! Synchronicity continues. I smile when he tells me his first name. Of course!

"Could it be any other?" I think to myself.

Dr. David begins to examine me while the other doctors ask questions. He helps me stand up and barely taps his finger against my chest. I fall over as the other doctors catch me. There is no resistance. I have no strength. I tell them about the blood that has been coming up for five days. I tell them about the coughing and I keep fading in and out. Sometimes I hear people and sometimes I don't know where I am. I tell them about the sherpas carrying me on their backs to the plane.

They ask me if I had any headaches or nausea? No. I have been taking the altitude sickness pills prescribed to me.

Dr. David begins. "We very seldom see your type of case. By the time the people get to us in the condition you are in, they are dead. You are suffering from high altitude pulmonary edema (HAPE) and high-altitude cerebral edema (HACE). You were bleeding like hell internally and didn't understand the significance and danger of it!" He asked me what size the blood clots were and I point to my fingertip, indicating most of the tip. He and the others shake their heads. He tells me I probably have mental confusion. I respond by nodding my head. He tells me the pills I have been taking have masked the symptoms of altitude sickness. Internal bleeding occurs with HAPE and HACE, a coma within hours and death within a day or two if the patient is not removed from the high altitude.

Dr. David looks at me intently and says, "sheer will got you to the top of that mountain to meet the Lama. Sheer will, through the sherpas, brought you back to safety." I don't tell them about the angels and the white satin cord. Would they think I was hallucinating? It doesn't make any difference. Yes, my intention and the sherpas' love brought me full circle. And through all of it were the angels and the power of the white satin cord. Those little angels with green wings and white wings made the difference. They went beyond the call of duty. The angels and the white satin cord helped me reach the mountain top, and the sherpas, who are also angels, helped get me back safely.

The doctors want blood tests and x-rays so Santi and her father drive me to the x-ray center. We spend most of the day in the medical clinic or the x-ray center. I have never seen people with so much patience. Santi and her father are always smiling. No, they don't mind waiting. I'm still learning. Maybe I can go back to the United States and be less demanding of people, and of time. Watching these people, I realize how much I admire them. Patience is a real virtue, and the Nepalese practice it as part of their daily lives. I have so much to learn. We return to the medical clinic, x-rays in hand. The blood test results are in. I am still a very sick lady. The doctors put me on antibiotics and they want me in bed immediately. Although I want to go back to the United States, they advise me to stay in Kathmandu for another day or two. I tell them Santi will take care of me, and she nods.

Santi and her father get me back to the sherpa lodge and into bed. I seem to sleep for hours. The night is more comfortable for me and my need for sleep is satisfied. Santi serves wonderful hot tea in the morning. As always, she is smiling. I am beginning to eat more solid food today. She brings me oatmeal. I continue to sleep nonstop for hours. I awake and find it is my second full day back in Kathmandu. I'll be leaving tomorrow morning for Bangkok on a flight that will bypass Seoul, Korea. It sounds like my flight will be much easier going home. Maybe my lessons will stop being so hard now. My American friends are not back yet. They are expected tomorrow, but my flight may leave before they come in. I hope we have a chance to connect one more time. I need to acknowledge their offer of financial support, and I hope I have the opportunity to say good-bye and wish them well.

I have asked J.P. if I can leave my thirty-pound duffle bag at the lodge with most of my stuff. I will carry my backpack with just a few things in it. I don't have the strength to carry much and I don't want to worry about baggage. He agrees. He will send it back to the states with someone from my area in California. I smile to myself. I wonder if I have left something behind at other places? Is there a part of me that doesn't want to leave? Yes, there is a part of me that will remain in Nepal. The walking sticks, comfortable hiking boots and warm wool sweaters are symbols that saw me through the hard parts.

Santi and her father are driving me to the airport this morning, and I am disappointed the other Americans haven't shown up yet. We pull out of the driveway and head down the street. Oh! Here they come. The Americans are here. We make a U-turn and head back to the lodge. My friends ask me how I am. I tell them Dr. David's diagnosis. Bill tells me the sherpas got back to Namache and could not talk about anything else for the rest of the week. He was sure they were still talking about it. It was an amazing experience for them and probably for me as well. Bill said Nima was still having a hard time breathing. I nod silently. Amazing is putting it lightly. Amy asks me what it was like to be carried in a basket? Tears begin to well up in my eyes again. I can't talk about it. Not now. Maybe not ever.

We hug and say our goodbyes. The four Americans will always have a place in my heart. Like the sherpas, they, too, are kind and caring human beings. I was blessed to be with their Light in our climb to the top of the world. I thank them for offering their money for the helicopter. Accepting their offer was not a choice for me. I would not have put my friends in such a vulnerable situation while trekking down the mountain. They needed their money. The sherpas were willing to carry me and that was the best way to get me out.

J.P. has told us to take the van rather than the car, now that it is back. We are climbing into the van and getting ready to pull out. Whoops! My backpack is in the car. Didn't this happen to me a couple of weeks earlier? This is different. I am the one who instantly realizes it is missing, and we recover it in a moment. Full circle and synchronicity are all part of the same. No hard lessons here.

We drive through the busy city of Kathmandu to the airport. It is a special city. The energy is high and connective. Everything seems so connected here. I say a silent prayer. Thank you, God, for giving me the chance to feel the connective grace of your people here. I bow to the Light in each one. I bow to the Lama and his Light. I bow to my own Light. I feel connected and I am beginning to feel whole and I am not the Jerri I once was. I am better - much better.

The Royal Thai Airways flight takes off without incident. It is a beautiful airline. I am resting comfortably and beginning to eat more although my slacks are still hanging on me. I haven't been this thin in years. I have a few hours to reflect on my life and observe what has brought me to this point. I lean back and close my eyes.

My mother had a very difficult delivery. We both almost died. She has RX negative blood and I have positive. Asthma and pneumonia were serious problems for me during my childhood years. I don't remember my father as an alcoholic when I was small. He functioned fine throughout my growing up years. I remember him as a very gentle and sweet man with a tough exterior. Maybe I took on more of his characteristics than I realized. He was a wonderful man with some obvious limitations, so I would have difficulty calling him an angel. However, in spite of those limitations, I was blessed to be his daughter. There were the hard moments. In my twenties, I had him committed to an alcohol detoxification unit in a county hospital. I carried out a family intervention thirty years before family interventions were found to be effective. The problem is, I did it alone. Eventually my decision to do that brought us even closer because the pretending stopped and the honesty began. But he died a year later in a hospital in my arms. He died of alcoholism. Over the years, I have known there was nothing I could have done to stop my father from drinking. I had tried everything and nothing worked. My father was the only one who could have done something. No one else.

That was several years after I had already experienced two divorces. I was raising my daughter alone. It was a couple of years before I experienced the sexual harassment, or should I say sexual assault and rape. It was before I nursed my daughter back to life after her near fatal car accident. Five years ago, I was diagnosed with an epilepsy disorder. That was a year after the head-on car collision, and three months before a bus hit me in a crosswalk. My trip to Nepal was important. I no longer have to live a hard life. I can choose the easy path. I can feel it happening in this moment.

My arrival in Bangkok is uneventful, a welcome relief. No one from the Department of Immigration greets me, but that may be because I have my passport. Captain Tik is nowhere to be found, but then, I am not looking for him. I go through customs easily and then to my hotel room. I will rest until tomorrow morning when my Delta flight leaves on December 31st. Because of the international dateline though, I will be celebrating two New Year's Eves. Out with the old and in with the new twice!

What a great way to begin the new year. I am resting, but the anticipation I'm feeling about going home is getting the best of me. I decide on a walk around the shops in the hotel lobby, and I am struck by the way I am walking. Each footstep is gentle and quiet. I am walking more easily and softly than I ever have before. I feel light. I wonder if this will last?

I see a small emerald green heart-shaped ring in the jewelery store window that reminds me that I left part of my heart in Nepal, and maybe even Bangkok. I decide to purchase it. I will carry my mandala necklace as a symbol of full life circle and I will glance at my finger and think of the heartfelt memories I have for Nepal and its people. Neither the necklace or the ring are very expensive. Just reminders of several moments in time that changed my life.

As I carry my lightweight backpack into the airline terminal, a Delta airline pilot and stewardess ask if they can go first. They have to catch a scheduled flight. I smile. Sure, they can go first. I remember two other Delta airline employees who were absolute angels to me. Maybe I will buy them little gold angel lapel pins and mail them when I get home. The pilot and stewardess place their bags on the security conveyor belt, look back at me and smile. Full circle is present.

Synchronicity continues to show itself in every movement of my life. Didn't I ask to go first at the security gate running to my Delta flight in San Francisco? Everyone was so gracious except the security gate guard, who was simply doing her job. But at least I don't have to contend with her now. Our tyrants can be our greatest teachers. The guard taught me I no longer want to be in power struggles. Life is too short and sweet for that.

I am picking up my backpack off the security console as a very official lady with a clipboard approaches me. "Yes, my name is Jerri Curry." Who is she? She tells me she is here to escort me through the terminal and to my flight and make my departure from Bangkok as easy as possible. Is Big Brother watching? I look around the terminal wondering who else knows me? She tells me it is not necessary to wait in the Delta ticket line. She will take care of it for me. She takes my ticket to the counter. She brings it back stamped and ready for my immediate use at the airline gate. Now we will need to stop by the immigration office and confirm possession of my passport. She laughs and speaks in a light and friendly manner. She is happy she can make it easy for me. Yes, she uses the word "easy". Immigration barely bats an eye at my departure. No problem. I may leave Bangkok on my Delta flight. This nice lady escorts me to the gate, and walks with me onto the plane and finds my seat. I tell her I will write a letter to her boss for her efforts. She gives me her name and says she appreciates the offer. I keep my word; I always do. Nothing is new about me in that regard. We give each other a hug. Is this what easy is? We won't be stopping in Seoul, Korea. There are no more lessons there. We will stop in Taipei for a short time, and then it will be nonstop to the United States.

Sitting in the Taipei airport waiting area is not difficult, just interesting. Sitting on the ledge near the window, I notice there is a little girl and her mother sitting next to me. I look down at the cheap wrist watch I am wearing that I had bought specifically for this trip. I have no need for it any longer. I offer it to the mother, as the little girl's face lights up. Unfortunately, she is not a trusting woman. I know what that feels like. Her eyes look suspicious and she shakes her head and pulls her daughter closer to her. I apologize if I've offended her. That was not my intention. She gets up and takes her daughter to another part of the terminal. I am sorry that I offered the gift. I just thought the child would enjoy it. I am too close to the experience to understand the message. Everything speaks to me so maybe it will come later.

We board our plane to the United States. I am heading home. It is time to begin my new life. This has been a mystical time. It has been a magical time. I am settled comfortably in my seat as we take off.

We have been in the air for a while and I notice a father with a son sitting nearby. I decide to try it again. I ask the father, out of earshot from the son just in case he also says no, if he'd like this watch for his son. I explain it is a cheap one and I bought it simply to wear while I was trekking in the Himalayas. I won't wear it at home. The father smiles genuinely and accepts the gift. He calls his son over and places it on his wrist. The little boy's eyes light up and he is told to thank me. I tell him he is welcome. I smile as I return to my seat. I don't know if it means anything. The feminine distrust and the masculine receptiveness may fit somewhere in this lesson. The message of balance is here. But rather than dissect the experience, maybe I will just enjoy the glow of the little boy's smiling eyes as he looks up at me.

I close my eyes and remember a few other mystical moments that have involved children and also reflects synchronicity.

In April 1981, my friend Beverly and I attended a week-long spiritual retreat. In the opening exercise, we were all asked to lie on the carpet so that our heads pointed toward the center. I felt the vibration of the music moving throughout my body and as I relaxed, I enjoyed the pictures as they flashed through my mind's eye.

I saw a leaf floating on a quiet stream gently turning in the breeze as it drifted by. I became that leaf. As I looked toward the sky, I saw an old World War II bomber flying overhead. The next thing I knew I was in the plane flying under a rainbow. Then I saw a stairway made of solid light-colored steps leading to a huge wooden double door with brass handles. I saw myself walking up the stairs, and once I arrived at the door, I began to knock.

A voice said I would need to know who I was before I could enter. So I physically checked out my entire body - every mole, every hair and every part of me. Once I had done so completely, the doors opened and I walked through.

Immediately I saw myself standing outside a farmhouse, looking through a kitchen window. Inside, a woman in a paisley dress was cooking at a wood stove. Children sat around the table and the woman said, "Jimmy, sit down and finish eating...you kids have got to get to school!" It was my father as a little boy.

In my vision, I could tune into any day of his life. I saw him skipping rocks across a pond and I saw him skipping school. I watched him grow up and saw him marry my mother. I observed their early years together, and watched as they gave birth to each of their children. I watched my own birth, and knew I could tune into any day of my life. I reviewed what I wanted to and then came to a day in my adult life when the Light was spiraling out the top of my head toward the center of the universe and was connected with the central Light. All Lights were streaming toward this world from the center, just like the Circle of Rainbow Light photograph taken, twelve years later, in the Himalayas.

At the end of the meditation, my Light beamed back to earth from the center and showered a small blonde-haired, blue-eyed boy. I was puzzled. I told the retreat group about the meditation but I didn't know any little boy who resembled the one I had seen.

What was I supposed to do with this vision? I was in school, having recently received my degree in public administration, and now I was working on a graduate degree. At that time I wasn't yet working with children and didn't have specific plans to do so.

Six years later, in 1987, after I had been working as a therapist for a couple of years, a woman telephoned and asked if I could see her family in therapy. Her six-year-old stepson had been alone with his natural mother when she died, and he was traumatized. I will call him Cory.[1]

At the first session, Cory was out of control. He hit and kicked everything in sight. During the session, I knelt on the floor so I could meet him at his level. As Cory stood behind his father's legs, I said, "Cory, earlier you said you were sorry when you kicked me, and it was the nicest 'I'm sorry' I have ever received. Thank you."

Cory, a blonde-haired, blue-eyed six-year-old, came out from behind his father. He walked toward me, put his arms around my neck and began to cry.

In a follow-up session, Cory and his stepsister, Christy, decided to draw a picture for me. It was a united effort, and as Cory was drawing an old World War II bomber, Christy drew a rainbow. Together, they drew a flower with one leaf on a stream.

I sat speechless, as I watched my meditation of six years earlier come to life. Then I wondered to myself silently, where is the ray of Light?

Just at that moment, Cory drew the sun with streams of Light coming down and Christy drew balloons floating toward the heavens. These little angels drew exactly what I had seen in my vision six years earlier.

When their parents returned to pick the children up, Cory and Christy excitedly showed them the picture. All of a sudden, Christy said, "Cory, you didn't put wings on the plane!"

"Yes, I did!", Cory insisted. "They're white. See, they are *angel* wings."

Cory had used a white crayon and had indeed, drawn angel wings. The drawing hangs in my office in a very special place.

If we open our eyes and hearts, we can see angels everywhere. Is there any coincidence that I saw Cory six years earlier in my meditation and that he was six-years-old when I met him? Or that Cory, in his teen years, continues to show an interest in World War II bombers?

I gave up believing in coincidences many years ago.

Daylight streams through the windows of the airplane cabin. We are arriving in Portland, Oregon. I will need to change planes, but my strength has returned and I am only carrying my light backpack, so there won't be a problem. I now find myself sitting in the airline's private lounge near a window overlooking the airport terminal lobby. People are carrying suitcases. They are greeting each other with hugs and crying with their goodbyes. Separation is the hardest lesson in life. Some of these people standing beneath me are experiencing this lesson. I feel I am watching a microcosm of society. There are people who are standing at the snack bar being nurtured and filled. Others are racing about as if they trying to catch up with their lives or someone else's. Children are holding balloons and looking up with innocent and smiling faces. The elderly support one another as they walk toward their destinations. Young lovers hold hands and wipe tears from each other's eyes as they part. Life continues for us all. I wonder how my life has changed. I am glad I will have the opportunity to experience the changes. I know I will never be the same again.

The flight to San Francisco is short and simple. The Delta reservation clerk is now looking for my infamous New Year's Eve bag, which actually turns up. Yes, my passport, my traveler's checks, my Nepal visa, J.P.'s name and address, my nylons, skirt and jeweled sweater, make up and curling iron are safe and secure. Where were you when I needed you? But having the purse was not part of the plan and I take in a deep breath as I feel every moment of the plan coming to an end now. That was when I expected everything to be hard. That no longer has to be and I know it. I feel it. I plan to live it.

It is New Year's Eve 1993. I celebrated it on the flight and I am celebrating it again in my home. I have a fire in the fireplace and I am sipping a glass of wine. A toast to my safe return. I cannot telephone anyone. I know my family and friends will want to hear from me, but I am home early so they won't expect a call for a few more days. I didn't send a postcard or letter throughout the trip. That isn't like me, but it was as if I was in a different world, not just a different country. I need time alone. I need time to think through what I've experienced.

It is January 2, 1994 and I have been home for a day and a half. Reading the Sunday paper, I casually turn to the feature section. I can't believe my eyes! What am I reading? Where did this come from? It is an article entitled **Saving the Sherpa Life**[2] by Molly Moore. Who saved whose life? Interesting choice of titles. It was written about my Tengboche Monastery, His Holiness the Lama and my sherpas. No, I don't know the author and I could not have known she was writing this article. It brings me close to those I have just left in Nepal. Synchronicity continues to reveal its magical moments. I see it in all things. Everything speaks to me.

Oh yes, before leaving for Nepal, I bought my friends and family members angel calendars. I looked at mine wondering how will 1994 be for me? I don't believe it will be a difficult year. I am through having hard years or a hard life. I left that in Bangkok and at the altar in the monastery. I brought with me the white silk scarf the Lama had placed around my shoulders. I want that blessing to be with me. I left the hard times behind. A thought passes through swiftly. I wonder if the candle globe is still burning at the altar. I have traveled half way around the globe and, if we choose, the world can continue to be bright with our Light.

It is a quiet Sunday. I am still amazed at the **San Francisco Examiner** article. One of these days synchronicity may not amaze me, but secretly I hope not, because there would be fewer rainbows in my life. I love living in magic. It is clear to me that miracles occur constantly. Biblical times did not have a monopoly on miracles. Once we realize synchronicity is present, it allows us to view the world and people differently. Just picking up a newspaper and reading it with synchronicity and the universal law of connection is an enlightening experience. The messages are loud and clear and we can hear them if we are in harmony with nature, humanity, our bodies, and the connections of all living things.

It is early evening and I am reading a book my friend Diane bought me for Christmas last year. **Ask your Angels**[3] (Daniels, Wyllie and Ramer, 1992) discusses the importance of angels and their existence. Angels, it says, may be "shafts of light, spirals of light, cones of light, ranging in size from a dot to a galaxy...If your subtle senses are fully developed, as they will be in your future history, you might begin to see (angels) as radiant pulsing beings of Light. This light isn't the same light that comes from a sun, a fire or a light bulb. It is a far more subtle and all-pervading Light."

We are on the brink of incredible spiritual changes and the transformation will be felt by everyone. Because we are so globally connected, the next dimension of awareness is emerging. Angels are experienced according to individual free will and there is no right way to be in their presence. We can choose how to interpret them and in whatever way we can, we fit their reality into our frame of reference.

Within a day, and without knowing why the urgency, I have the film from my disposable little paper camera developed at the local film processing shop. I want to see the mountains and to remember the new friends I have left behind. The pictures are beautiful. Mt. Everest is wonderful. I don't understand two of the pictures though. A spot of light appears in the lower left hand corner of one picture and a circle of light in another. I cannot interpret what they mean.

Later in the week I find myself at a Buddhist meditation center for an evening of meditation with similar-minded people. I run into a friend who is a professional photographer. I am puzzled by these two photos; can she explain what they are? She doesn't know, but asks if I have the negatives. Yes, *by accident*, and I use those words loosely, they are in my car. I bring them into the building and she looks at the negatives in the light. Her response, "I don't know what it is, Jerri. There is nothing in the negative that would cause this light. Maybe it is an Angel." I blink. I think I have just expanded my frame of reference.

In meditation I am becoming fully aware of what I have been through. My dominating, aggressive spirit and will to succeed got me to the top of the mountain, literally the mountain and in my life. The struggles have been enormous. The surrender through trust and the willingness to receive allowed me to go down the mountain and create a life of harmony and balance. It was a magical, mystical moment in time.

I take my two negatives to a professional color lab so transparencies can be made. The technicians, Steve and Alex, find the process perplexing and unexplainable, and have "never had this type of photo negative problem before".[4] They spend an extraordinary amount of time trying to work with the "density" of the negatives, and for a while, their equipment is no match for the density (Light) which is in them. Alex and Steve explain it to me,

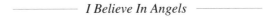

"There is too much Light in the photographs... and there is no explanation for it...it is not overexposure and our equipment went to the extreme to match the light in the negatives."

It is clear to me that miracles continue to occur constantly. Once we realize synchronicity is present, it allows us to view the world and people differently. Then our lives can be filled with double rainbows rather than the grayness of life. The messages are loud and clear and I feel more in tune with the wonders of nature, of my self and of the connection of all living beings.

Some may say my experiences are based on magical thinking. That is a psychological term often heard in the mental health field. The magical thinking explanation allows a spiritual or peak experience to fit comfortably within a certain frame of reference. Others may say I might have a personality or character disorder in explaining my mystical experiences. As a result of my educational requirements, the work I do, and the accident years ago, I have undergone comprehensive psychological testing. All the teachers, doctors and their tests summed it up simply through one doctor's statement, "You are the most normal person I have ever evaluated." It took a long time to be comfortable with the moments in my life, but that foundation is now firmly established and I know the reality of the experiences.

As Carl Jung believed, it is through the integration of the self that we can begin to experience the whole of the community and the world, and the Oneness of life.

Another beacon in the field of psychology was Abraham H. Maslow (1978). He believed peak experiences are not necessarily magical thinking and made the following comments: *"...after the insight or the great conversion...great mystical experience...full awakening, one can calm down as the novelty disappears...he can't really become naive or innocent again or ignorant in the same way he was."*

And the Buddhist believes that through struggle and experience, enlightenment comes to a person. Throughout history, man has revealed unexplained mystical experiences in which his life is dramatically transformed. William James (1902) said, *"all religious experience has its roots in the mystical experience and... in mystic states we both become one with the Absolute and we become aware of our Oneness."*

Sherap and I write to one another often. He tells me that he went to Bhutan to visit with his family immediately after our trek together. He felt the need to connect, too. Synchronicity in its most subtle moments. In a letter he uses the word, "separate," but does not spell it correctly. Perhaps he is not familiar with the word just as I was not familiar with the word, sajilo, which means "easy" in Nepalese. He has asked me not to forget my Nepali friend and wants to know when I will be returning to the Himalayas so he can serve me again. I have given each sherpa a one year's salary in gratitude for their serving me so beautifully. Perhaps someday Sherap will come to the United States. He wants to do that. I write and tell him that clear intention is all anyone needs, and then everything is possible. He already knows that. He lives it.

The sherpas offered me a new way of looking at life, while his Holiness the Lama gave me the wisdom that allows me to live my life with ease. He also gave me the gift of recognition by seeing who I truly am. I hope I can give others the space and respect to express who they are. I learned from the best, but that doesn't mean I will be perfect in doing it. It does mean it is my intention to bring that teaching into my life and practice it with those I encounter, know and love.

I am moving toward wholeness in recognizing nothing stays the same and knowing every universal movement is interconnected and this is the reality of life. Buddhists teach us to forget the self. I begin an affirmation, "this is not about me," and that removes the personal hurt of another or feeling misused by others. I find myself saying that many times a day, and it releases me from blaming myself. It doesn't mean I am not responsible for what I do, but only that I don't have to carry the fault of others on my shoulders. Most things are not about me and everyone needs to be accountable for their own decisions and their acts. It is another way of saying I just need to get out of my own way by letting go of self-importance, power struggles, taking up space that rightfully belongs to others and my failure to recognize the Light in others. It is easy to list these *getting in the way* issues because I have lived with many of them most of my life.

Carol Lee Flinders (1993), the author of **Enduring Grace** describes some who have had mystical moments like this:

> *"(It's) Turbulence, in any event, and sorrow of a great many kinds...from beginning to end: ill health, overwork, and exhaustion, political opposition, alienation from friends or loved ones...the grief and turmoil of their lives is that the impression they leave with us is ultimately one of joy and transcendence...(they) know sorrow and disappointment inside and out, but they had also made their peace with them...have healed that division; everything about them conveys wholeness, and inclusion."*

Mystical experiences do not have to be near death experiences or other extraordinary moments. My nephew Darren said he saw something very unusual coming through a building while driving in a small European village. I asked him if it had anything to do with a White Light and he said he wasn't sure, but that it was, maybe, "like a flashbulb going off". I told him that sounded like the White Light to me. He said it will have a lasting effect on his life. A friend named Jeff said he was in a relaxation exercise when he saw a Light coming through a porthole. He was drawn to the Light and it changed his life. My stepfather said he was once on a tugboat, fell between two boats and yelled to his friend, Ted, "help me. The ladder is falling." Ted grabbed his hand and yelled back, "I'll break my arm before I drop you." My stepfather said he remembers their hands together more than any other part of the experience. Hands clasp and the connection is made once again.

I tell a friend about a dream I had the night before and he tells me not to pay it any attention. It was probably just my subconscious trying to manipulate a certain outcome, he says. I shake my head as I drive away from our meeting place. A car passes me and the bumper sticker reads, "**Listen to your Dreams**." Synchronicity, like ripples in a pond, one reaching out touching the other. It is a constant.

Weeks later I am on my car phone talking with my mother. She tells me she is getting letters and phone calls from family members who have been away from her for months. This news warms my heart. I think, "My mother is making important connections." A car drives by with a license frame that reads, "**Good connections**." I shake my head in constant wonderment. This plan is much greater than I can imagine. It is far beyond my frame of reference and I probably still won't really understand until beyond this lifetime.

I do see the bond building between people of this world. A bond of certainty, a bond of beauty, a bond of friendship and support. People within this world, and perhaps beyond, have reached out toward one another now more than ever before. This reaching out will be felt throughout the universe and be far greater than any other time in the history of mankind. Everyone will want to connect and be part of the Wholeness. I see beyond the reality of this world and my new life emerges through awareness and intention to be with the compassionate universal spirit.

---

[1]To keep confidentiality, all of the names have been changed.

[2]**The San Francisco Examiner** feature article published with permission from the **Washington Post** by Molly Moore, dated January 2, 1994.

[3]Timothy Wyllie and I met at the American Booksellers Convention in Los Angeles in the Spring of 1994. He offered to write an endorsement of **I Believe in Angels**. I consider it an honor and his endorsement is a valuable addition to my story.

[4]The **Ziba Color Lab** in San Francisco wrote a letter attesting to the unusual amount of density, i.e., Light, coming from the negatives and that their equipment had to be pushed to the extreme to match the negative. Once the transparencies were made, Alex and Steve heard the story behind the photograph, and then Steve, with emotion, said he saw the angel in his equipment. He asked me to make sure and protect the negatives. I am doing so with all my heart and my soul.

 CHAPTER SEVEN: **GOODBYE STRUGGLE, HELLO EASE**

1994 was a year of practicing new patterns and not repeating old ones. Struggles had become a pattern in my life. And when I felt like I was losing the struggle, I became more aggressive in my attempt to win. Now I know winning isn't that important. Letting go of struggles and keeping my integrity is. For a long time I denied my truth and my value. For example, prior to leaving for Nepal, there was a ruthless individual who owed me a lot of money, and for several years I had tried to collect it through the judicial system. There were times when I would *give up* and try to go away like a *good little girl*. I even attempted to give the money away by turning the judgment over to my attorney, and it was only after that offer was rejected that I learned money is a symbol of value and self-worth. So I couldn't give it away anymore. I had done that for too long and too often.

The way I handle difficult situations is very different since returning from Nepal. I continue to express my truth, but if at all possible, now I do it with *compassion*. Such a simple word and yet it has strength, if practiced. I saw the compassion in the Lama's eyes. It was a mirror for me and one that I carry as part of my soul. I also didn't understand the difference between being a good girl and being feminine. Now I do. If I need to confront an injustice, I have learned to do that with a softness and directness I did not have before Nepal. I have begun to reach beyond myself by learning that aggressiveness or anger prevents me from acknowledging the God essence in others.

That includes the ruthless one. Being spiritual doesn't mean stuffing my feelings and allow others to violate my worth. It means keeping my integrity and expressing myself in the most authentic and gentle way possible. It is not my intention to hurt anyone in that process. It is my intention to have clear communication and fair resolution without compromising my self-worth and power.

I had learned to express a certain sense of power after feeling abused and betrayed by men. However, until Nepal, I did not realize it was a false sense of power, not my true essence, and that it did not reflect the real power I possess. Outwardly, as an adult, I expressed false power by becoming arrogant and forceful. I am learning that my real power is my quiet and receiving presence. That allows me to place a high value on myself and to maintain the integrity of my soul. I have a better understanding of separation and connection and the significance of both.

For some time I had a serious separation from my daughter and my grandson. It was a painful time in my life. The first separation was when I almost lost my daughter in an automobile accident. The second separation was caused by both of us. Separation is the hardest lesson in life. This past year, my daughter Kathleen and I came together again. I treasure her and our friendship. We talk more honestly now. I learned to trust that my daughter would find her own way, and that's what she seems to be doing. I, too, am on my chosen path. That gives us the more positive relationship we have today.

We have talked through some of our differences and are closer than we were before our self-imposed separation. I missed her and my grandson greatly. She said they missed me. We baked Christmas cookies together during Christmas, 1994. I am not traveling this year. I am at home and I am happy.

I have had the opportunity to honestly validate and recognize my mother and my daughter on several occasions, and those moments have strengthened our bonds.

It is my challenge in evolving to my highest good to experience separation with grace and dignity. That will free me to move into the total connection with all of life. I now know the only thing I own is my soul, and with free will I have chosen to share my soul with the universe. I have learned to handle separation with greater dignity and truth. It is my feeling there will be few tough separation experiences in the coming years. Now, and in my future, enjoying the abundance of connections will be the hallmark of my life. I am still learning how to treat everyone and everything the same. Even though it is a wonderful theory, it is hard to practice, but my intention is clear.

It is not always up to just one person when reaching out. Both people must make the effort toward connection. I have surrendered to several painful separations during my life. With that surrender has come peace and more solid relationships with my family and my friends. Separations are important to spiritual development. The metaphor of Adam and Eve teaches the original sin of separation. They chose the apple and were separated from God, and since then our lesson is separation, and ultimate connection. My separations were extremely hard, but now I understand the learning behind each one. It has allowed me to learn my lessons and to evolve toward wholeness. Am I whole yet? Spiritual evolvement is a process; there is no beginning and there is no ending. I know in my heart that I truly know nothing other than the fact that I do own my soul. The most important law of free will confirms that. Still I continue to learn.

My mother and I have the best friendship I could ever want. We have fun together and I am blessed to have her and my stepfather, Harry, in my life as friends. They are good people.

My special Aunt Virginia, with whom I lived during the summers of my high school years, is also in my life and she continues to be a second mother to me. Her sister, my Aunt Louise, was 91 this year and we celebrated it together. I enjoy Virginia's grandchildren. Her nine-year-old great grandson, Cody, upon seeing the angel picture, reprimanded me and said, "Jerri, you aren't supposed to take a picture of an angel!". I nodded and said, "You might have a good point, Cody. But what happens if the angel just shows up in the picture without asking for permission?" He nodded, and agreed that might be a problem.

Prior to Nepal, patience was not one of my virtues and the intense, demanding part of my personality was a big part of my shadow. Watching Santi and her father at the medical clinic in Kathmandu wait for me for hours was a learning experience. I remember facing my fear of missing my plane as I rounded the corner at the San Francisco Airport. I saw the long line of people waiting to go through the security gate, and my fear was unmanageable. My patience was nowhere to be found and the security guard pointed that out over and over again.

Another part of my shadow was my inability to allow others their own emotional space. My energy took up all the room. I must have left a lot of resentment in my tracks and I wasn't even aware of it, at least not consciously. That does not mean my Light needs to be any dimmer. It just points out the need to have the sensitivity to leave the space for others to express their Light. I felt that during our meeting with the Lama. There were hundreds of questions I could have asked him, but I chose only two. It was important to leave room for those around me. I knew how to initiate, but through fear I would not receive. The sherpas gave to me over and over again during our five-hour struggle to the plane. They gave more to me than I could ever have received before; they were my teachers. My vulnerability and openness were not betrayed by these five men, and for that I am grateful. I now know there are people who are safe and sensitive, especially in our most vulnerable moments, and I have learned with love to receive.

While the sherpas carried me on their backs, the sounds of their feet were heavy as they carried me and my burdens. The experience reminds me of the prayer in which the person is complaining that when he and Jesus were walking on a beach, Jesus' footprints were missing when the times were the hardest. Jesus' voice comes back and says, "I didn't leave you; that was when I carried you". Jesus Christ was an important part of my childhood, and my thoughts return to him now. He must have been an all inclusive person and been many things to many people. He could be a part of Mohandas Gandhi, Mother Teresa, the hero who saves the drowning victim, the fireman who runs into a burning building to save a child, or five sherpas who carry a woman to a new life. I don't think it enhances our respect for Jesus Christ to get stuck on semantics. The Buddha taught wise words to many faithful followers; his life was much like that of Jesus Christ. The God I know is all inconclusive because God is limitless and does not know separation.

Upon my return from Nepal, I found it took me several weeks to talk about the trip. As time went on I found a need to write about the connections I had made while in Nepal. But I struggled with the idea of writing about me. I told my friend Diane that it sounded pretty egotistical to write such a book. She said, "Get out of your own way, Jerri. The book is about the experiences in your life, not necessarily you. The experiences need to be shared." That is what I am doing. This is not about me and it is about experiences in life.   As a former victim, I used to say, "What did I do wrong? Poor me." Now I simply say, "This is not about me." I continue to be accountable for my own behavior but not for everyone else's. It has been a statement of freedom that has released me from being a victim. Taking on the role of victim is easy and letting go of that role is difficult. I know because it took me years and my lessons with the Lama, to learn a healthier, and happier way of living life. There are payoffs in being a victim. I got attention and I got sympathy. Now I don't need either.

During a meditation, I learned that July 15, 1994, was the day I would mail out my book proposal for **I Believe In Angels** to several publishers I had met at a Los Angeles conference. The week of July 15th was stressful because of my effort to meet the deadline. I worked night and day through July 15th. At 5:00 p.m. on that day, I realized I was not going to get the book proposal down to the post office on time. Meeting deadlines and reaching goals is important to me and nothing was going to get in the way of that happening.   It was much like meeting the Lama at the Monastery on Christmas Day. Some things in me will never change.

On July 15, 1994, at 7:30 p.m., I race to the copy shop and have three copies made of the original book proposal. I have them bound and take them to a restaurant where I am waiting for take out food. I haven't eaten all day. I am ready to put the book proposals in the addressed envelopes and mail them after I leave the restaurant. I glance through the proposal while waiting for my dinner. Oh no, I can not mail this out! There are mistakes that we have not caught. It isn't ready to be mailed. As upset as I am, I now know I am not going to reach my goal on July 15th. I decide I won't die in failing to reach this goal. I am also learning about flexibility. If I don't become more flexible, there is less room to be receptive. I return home and stay up until 2:30 a.m. rewriting parts of the proposal.

It is Saturday morning, July 16th, and I telephone my editor and talk to her briefly. Then I rush out the door on my way to my office to see some clients, knowing that I won't have time to leave the manuscript at the copy shop on my way. I will have to take it by after work this afternoon. As I walk into my office, I say a little prayer. Lord, I have put so much energy and attention into this concept of connection in writing this book proposal, and I am not in a place today to listen to separating statements from people going through divorces and fighting over their children. Could you do me a favor and have the four people I am supposed to see today not have a need to meet with me? I then waited for the first person to show up and, lo and behold, he never did. Guess what? That is exactly what happened to all of my appointments. I had four hours to wait until my 2:00 p.m. appointment who did show up.

So I sat in my office and read my book proposal. Oh no, more mistakes! I will have to go home this afternoon and correct them. Good thing I didn't take it by the copy shop earlier today. That would have been a waste of money. I will go later this afternoon. Are the angels involved in these delays? And if so, why?

I spend the rest of the afternoon working on the final copy and I call the copy shop at 5:30 p.m., and ask the young man, "How late are you open?" He says, until 6:00 p.m., and I panic. I race through what I think are the finishing touches, and drive to the copy shop. I walk in and see a young man I have not worked with in the past. I feel uncomfortable having him help me. It is just a feeling. I trust my feelings all of the time since Nepal. I tell him he has a choice. It is ten minutes to six o'clock, and I know he closes at six o'clock. Does he want to take on this job that will take at least thirty extra minutes? When he responds, "no big deal", I immediately know he isn't in sync with this book. It is a very big deal! It has the *angels'* name on it. I tell him I will go to another copy place that is open twenty-four hours a day. I thank him and say good-bye. My inner voice continues to serve me well and I hear it much more clearly since Nepal.

I drive to a copy shop fifteen minutes away, and walk in and stand at the counter. I stand at the counter waiting for help but no one approaches me. One young man continues to wait on everyone else but not me. Before Nepal, I would have *demanded* attention. Now I just smile and say to myself, "I wonder why the angels don't want him to help me put this book proposal together?" I keep smiling and I keep waiting. A second man has said he will help me in a moment. I have been waiting thirty minutes. He approaches me, and I tell him I wished I was at home right then watching Pavarotti, Carreras and Domingo on the public broadcasting channel. The three greatest opera singers in the world coming together and connecting in the name of music. Isn't it grand! He said he would be back in a moment.

While waiting for him, a woman customer approaches the counter and reaches for my **San Francisco Examiner** article **"Saving the Sherpa Life"** dated January 2, 1994. She asks me what am I doing with the article. "I am writing a book proposal," I tell her. Glancing at her papers on the counter, I see the same six-month-old article, and I ask her what *she* is doing with it. She had lived at the Tengboche Monastery for two years, she says, and was very upset with the reporter who had gotten the Lama's name wrong. She was writing a letter to the newspaper. Oh, Oh. Obviously in my ill condition while at the monastery I had not gotten the correct spelling of the Lama's name, and I took the name from the news article rather than checking it with my friends in Kathmandu. That means the name is wrong in my book proposal! It is apparent I am not supposed to get it copied and bound right now. The angels want this to be a book that is accurate. I have to go home and change the manuscript. The second man returns to the counter and reaches for the book proposal. I grab it back and tell him I have to take it home and make some corrections thanks to the young woman standing next to me. Talk about losing my credibility. She must wonder how can I write a book when I don't even know the correct spelling of the Lama's name.

I drive home laughing all the way. The angels definitely want this book proposal to be done correctly. Their name is on it. No book of theirs will go out less than perfect, according to their standard of perfection. I arrive home in time to watch the **PBS** special and I change the book proposal too. I make two phone calls to Nepal and speak to Santi and then J.P. who give me another spelling of the Lama's name. However, there are so many interpretations from Nepalese to English that even then my spelling might be wrong. J.P. says the way we Americans spell Rinpoche is incorrect. He insists during our phone conversation that it is spelled Rimpoche. To this day, I still don't know the correct spelling and I may never know. I get off the phone and watch the show because the singing by Pavarotti, Carreras and Domingo is great, and I know the angels won't mind. I have a sense of certainty the proposal will be in the mail before midnight on July 16, 1994.

I return to the copy shop around 10:30 p.m. and wait for the second man to assist me. I stand at the counter and, again, I just smile. I wonder who the angels want to put this book proposal together? I also smile at my patience. It's such a difference in behavior for me when I can just observe what is going on rather than taking everything so personally and being so demanding. The delay isn't about me either. Very few things are about me. I have learned that since returning from Nepal. What freedom!

The universal story is unfolding all of the time if I allow myself to listen and look. Eventually the second man takes my book proposal and tells me someone will get to it. He places it on the counter and puts a yellow flag on it. I sit down just watching the unfolding human drama before my eyes. I find it fascinating. Everything speaks to me.

The first man, who earlier in the evening had ignored me, walks past on his way out the door as he heads for home. He stops and asks if I have been waited on, as if it was the first time he noticed me. I said I wasn't sure. My work project was sitting on the counter. He walks over and takes the yellow flag off and replaces it with a red one, which must have then labeled it a rush job. That is his part in this book process. He tells me he is going home but someone would get to it soon. The second man is nowhere to be found. I guess the angels don't want him to work on the printing job either.

A few minutes later, a young man named Michael comes into the shop and puts on a work apron with his name tag on it. He immediately walks over to the counter, looks at my project, and takes the red flag off and begins to copy the book proposal into seven sets. I approach the counter as he brings the finished copies toward me. I ask him for his advice. "Michael, if you were the publisher and were receiving this book proposal, how would you feel about seeing an angel sticker on the front of it?" Michael says not to do that. Then I tell him the importance of rainbows in the book and ask if he would divide the nine sections of the proposal with one solid color piece of paper or would he use different colors as dividers? He takes out a sample book and immediately opens it to one page that shows exactly nine soft pastel colors and suggest I use them. Yes, of course. That will be perfect. We smile at each other. He is open and receptive. The criteria needed for mystical moments. Once I learn the value of receiving, I do not forget it. I notice when it is missing in me and when it is present in others. I ask him if he wants to see a photograph of an angel. His eyes open wide and he says, "Yes!" I show him the picture, which he says his mother would love to see. Then he returns to the copy machine where he picks up the other copies. He asks me if I want a color photo of the angel picture. I tell Michael I don't need one, but perhaps he and his mother might. He smiles at me with his eyes. The photos are copyrighted, but they also need to be shared with other angels as often as possible. I knew this gift to Michael and his mother would be valued. Michael is certainly the one to be helping me. He is open enough to appreciate the significance of the angel photograph. He probably has double rainbows in his life too!

Michael returns to the counter with the angel copies. They are amazing! Absolutely beautiful colors of the angel! I had no idea the copies would look like they do. I also knew Michael would value this gift. The copy of the photo is with the rightful owner.

As Michael binds the seven book proposals, another man named Ronald walks in and puts on an apron. He approaches the counter and asks me what I am doing. I tell him about the book proposal and Nepal. He, too, is very open and willing to receive. He talks about his upbringing in the Jewish religion and I tell him I need advice from him. I tell him the book is about connecting and handling separation with grace and dignity, and I show him this paragraph in the book proposal:

> *"I have learned that in aligning myself to the greater will, alternately called unconditional love, the universe, the higher self, Prophet Mohammed, Jesus, Tao, the Buddha or any words which resonate, true strength is discovered."*

I say the missing part is the Jewish representative, and who would that be since I want to include it in this paragraph. "Abraham," he says, and he explains why Abraham is important for the Jewish faith. I tell Roger his information will be in the book and he smiles. I don't pretend to be a religious scholar, or even a well read spiritualist. I am just a normal person, doing the best I can, and living the best way I know how.

Michael and I finish the book bindings, and I begin to gather up my belongings and leave. It is ten minutes before midnight. Ronald returns to the counter and hands me a copy of a photograph. It is the monastery at Tengboche! I had been too ill to even think about taking any pictures while at the monastery. Not having the photograph had left a little empty space in my heart. I had wished I could have had a picture of the monastery since returning from Nepal. Here it is in my hands. My monastery! Our eyes meet and Ronald knows the importance of the gift to me. Earlier I had given Michael the gift of a photograph. Everything is so synchronized. Angels come in all shapes, sizes, forms, colors and religions. Is it strange this man has a picture of Tengboche? Not at all if you understand and accept synchronicity.

The men in the copy shop use their postage meter and put postage stickers on the packages with the July 16, 1994, postmark on them. I wave good-bye to my angels and walk out the front door. I know I will not have time to get to the post office, but there is no need for that now. I walk to the mailbox outside the copy place and drop the packages in the mail. Michael walks out, smiles and wishes me a good night. I wish him the same and thank him once again. We get in our separate cars and take different paths, knowing our meeting for a moment is part of divine order through the universe's plan of synchronicity. The plan never gets in the way of free will. How it all works continues to be a mystery to me, but work it does.

Before Nepal I might have looked at the weekend of July 15th as difficult, or at the very least, as a challenge. After Nepal, I look at it with simple awareness and amusement. Free will and openness allow for all possibilities.

Synchronicity abounds in every waking moment, in every breath, in every thought, in everything. It is how the universe was created. I see the connections in all things. Viewing the world from that position makes life a rainbow and full of feeling.

The Lama's message, "Treat everyone and everything the same" has been a part of my life since returning to the United States. I am sensitive to my own vibration in thought and action and sensitive to the energy of others. I choose not to be connected to a lower vibration, i.e., arguing with others versus sitting in a room with others in meditation. If I must be in that negative experience, my vibration will continue to be at my own deeper level of peace with the knowledge that total connection is the ultimate goal.

My past aggressiveness was reflected in the way in which I drove my car. It was also a reflection of how I used to live my life. I would be less than considerate to other drivers, perhaps cutting them off, going faster than I should and being very "hard" on my car and me and others on the highway. My car speaks to me too. It is symbolic of my choices and lifestyle. I call this "being more aware of the connections of all things." I am willing to learn from everything. If my car breaks down, I want to look at what part of my life is not working now. If I am in an accident, what destructive choices am I making and what path am I on that I need to change? It doesn't mean I caused the accident; it only means at some unconscious level I chose to be on that road when an opportunity to learn appeared. Every experience is an opportunity. If my car is stolen, what part of my emotional life has been taken or given away? I don't let that happen to me anymore.

I ended 1994 very differently than the way I started it. One experience that comes to mind was the purchase of a new car. I wanted to buy a car from a woman salesperson because that felt like honoring my femininity. That didn't happen because of a scheduling conflict with the saleswoman at the dealership. I then went to another car dealership that had very expensive cars that were beyond my budget, but I wanted to see what used cars they might have. I met Michael. He had the Light in his eyes. I felt it. Without bartering back and forth, within minutes there was an offer on the table for his boss. As he was writing up the offer he said he was going to add a car alarm system and floor mats. I thanked him for the offer. That was generous of him.

I was feeling a little sad because I had wanted to buy a car from a woman for the feminine part of my process, but business is business and this was a good business deal. Michael returned from his boss's office a few minutes later, and said the car was mine. "Robin has approved it." I asked him who Robin was and he said, "Oh, *she* owns the dealership." I smiled. I will experience my full femininity this year and it will be so powerful! *She owns it!* Michael told me, "You were very clear about what you wanted. It was *easy* to write up the offer." My purchase price for the new car was not as much as the price I had paid for a less luxurious car in 1988. When there is no struggle, I know I am on the right path. Magical thinking? No, just simple awareness and appreciation for the synchronicity of life.

There is a balance in my life that has not been there for a very long time; if ever. There is a master plan and it is far beyond anything I can comprehend. This master plan

includes free will and nothing violates that process. Connections come in the most unexpected moments. I connect through negative or positive intention. It is my choice and I wish to choose wisely. The goodness of each soul is always present though I may lose sight of that truth in my lowest or most vulnerable moments. The sherpas helped me see that showing my vulnerability does not mean I will be betrayed. It is in my vulnerability that I realize the full potential of my power. My spirit is in harmony with the Oneness of the world, and I am finally at my best. The lessons and opportunities will continue to come, but the difficulties seem to disappear. Life is easy and I am blessed for knowing this truth.

Recently it has come to my attention that my six-year-old grandson Danny's birthday is the same as my closest friend, Diane, whom I consider to be my sister. My other grandson, Chad, has a birthday on the same day as another close friend, Beverly, whom I consider as my other sister. Our friendships span over fifteen years. I share that information with my sisters and we all laugh together. Think of the things we miss in this grand master plan if we are closed to possibility. The connections come in the most unexpected ways.

Danny and I like spending time together, especially after being separated for several years. Our bond has always been strong, and never threatened, no matter what the outer circumstances. A few days before Christmas of 1994, Danny and I are sitting on the living room couch at his home. His Uncle Josh is caring for the baby, Chad, while I am with Danny. My daughter and son-in-law are out shopping for presents. Danny is tracing pictures from a book when he spontaneously looks at me and says, "G.G., I know what God's spirit is." I slowly look at my wise, old soul shaman and ask, "Danny, what is God's spirit?" He continues tracing as he says, "The rainbow." I ask Danny who told him that and he looks at me with an innocent smile and says, "No one. I just knew that by myself." A moment later, Danny says, "G.G., I know what else is God's spirit." I hesitate for just a moment, and say, "And what else is God's spirit?", and Danny responds, "Every person's name in the whole wide world; my first name and my last name and my middle name and everybody else's name in the world." Then he smiles and says, "G.G., I knew that by myself, too." Danny does not attend church or Sunday School. I think he did know it all by himself. I am in the presence of an angel. Maybe several.

On Christmas Day, 1994, Danny and I are sitting on the floor putting together a toy from Santa Claus. We are talking. Since our reunion, we are always talking. Our conversation is about "up there," also known as heaven versus "down there," also known as hell. He explains it to me. "G.G., down there means not being with anyone else. Nothing happens". I ask Danny about the devil. "There isn't a devil. You are alone all the time and you don't get anything". I ask Danny about God. Danny tells me "God sends us here." I ask him why. "Because it is fun," Danny responds. He is my teacher and I love the learning.

A year later as I am reading a new book entitled, **The Secret Language of Symbols** by Dr. David Fontana, I learn that the rainbow symbol has an even more significant meaning than I had given it.

> *"...In the Hindu and Buddhist Tantric traditions, the **rainbow body is the highest meditative state attainable.** The four elements that make up the body dissolve symbolically into rainbow light, and earthly life is shown to be truly insubstantial."*

I continue to learn about my fear too. Early on, I decide to have a professional photo lab make my Angel and the Circle of Rainbow Light[1] negatives into large poster size photographs. Fear surfaces: "What if they find out it is a spot or a cloud and not my angel?" The Angel and the Circle of Rainbow Light photographs are important and now I have an emotional investment in keeping the angel photograph in my life. Fear becomes our reality if we keep it. I freeze in that fear. I decide I won't have the posters made, but then I choose to meditate. My angel speaks:

> *"I have appeared to you for a reason. I am more real than most things on your earth. It is time to share the existence of our being so others can learn, be comforted and*

choose more wisely their tasks and actions at hand. The angels were with you in the Himalayas and we are with each of you now. Know this truth and feel our presence. There will be those who will know and feel our presence and those who will choose not to. Beyond the importance of connecting in the Light is the continuation of free will. It is with accepting and respecting free will that we will reach our highest good in connecting with the Light and becoming Whole."

The Angels continue to speak and to share. May your awareness and free will shower you with blessings in the experience of your Angels, and may your life be *fun and full of rainbows!*

---

[1]Recently I learned that there have been other photographs that are similar to the Circle of Rainbow Light (not necessarily with rainbows though) so there may be an explanation for that particular photo. However, the density of the photographs remains a mystery and the Angel photograph is, according to my free will, an Angel.

PROLOGUE: **LEARNING THE LAW OF SYNCHRONICITY**

As we enter the year 2000, our awareness and respect for synchronicity will be the experience of every moment. Individual thought, word and deed is intricately linked together with all universal thought, word and deed. Our consciousness of this link will allow us to treat everything and everyone the same, and live our lives with ease and more fully.

We are beginning to experience the scientific, economic, social, political, international, environmental, personal and religious realms of the world with the knowledge that everything speaks to us, and teaches us through interconnectedness. This is a world far beyond our current ability to comprehend, but we will come to know and experience this world through the understanding of synchronicity. The law of synchronicity is real whether it fits within our current frame of reference or not. When ideas and events go beyond our reality, we may minimize, deny or negate the existence of those ideas or events. We may do that out of fear. The definition of fear is *life denial*. Once we realize synchronicity is the universal law, we will experience the world and people without fear.

Separatists will no longer succeed in our world. When a political, governmental, social, religious, environmental, personal or intellectual decision is made that is inclusive rather than exclusive, the decision will be supported by the universal law and it will succeed. Exclusive decisions, concepts and ideas will fail without the support of the universe.

For instance, it is no accident that fission is slowly being replaced with fusion. Our movement from dependency on an energy that separates, to an energy that connects, is the focus of much scientific investigation today. What I find striking is that fission has in it an "i" to symbolize the individual, while fusion contains an "us", to symbolize unity. We no longer have to split the atom for energy; now we can bring it together for the energy we need. Fusion will succeed because it fits with the spiritual harmony of the universe as we become One.

Remember the two billion dollar super collider in Texas which became obsolete before it even got started? It, too, was based on the concept of splitting which is why the universe did not support its development.

The intercommunication global network is more of a reality than we thought possible a few short years ago. Internet connects many through the use of a tool which is relatively new to the human race: the computer. The computer is not within the frame of reference for many people in the world today. That doesn't mean that computers do not exist though.

It is a commonly held theory within the field of linguistics that "all human languages come from a common source".[1] There are rumors that the stock markets of the world are coming together. Are empires being made? Perhaps, but not if those empires exclude others. If an empire is focused on separating, that empire may temporarily experience power, but it will fall rapidly without connection.

Politically, NAFTA (North American Free Trade Agreement) is proving to be more successful than most could have imagined. The recently passed GATT (General Agreement on Tariffs and Trade) legislation in Congress will also be successful. It allows connection of international trade between many nations of the world; a symbol of connection. This is no surprise to those who understand the law of synchronicity.

In the past decade we have seen the separating walls of Germany and of Russia come to an end. Their struggles through years of separation created tremendous hardships for many. Separation is the hardest lesson in life and with heightened awareness it will no longer be part of future generations.

It is a heartfelt experience in watching the representatives of the PLO and Israel shake hands and smile. That coming together which supports the universal healing has taken so long to succeed. One of the most profound examples of a coming together this decade was the elimination of apartheid in South Africa.

Countries may all be united as One for we are one planet and one people. Honoring that reality allows us to have world harmony. There may be those who continue to struggle and fight for separation, but the greater challenge and higher vibration is to connect because separatists will no longer succeed in our society.

These opinions are not political. They are spiritual.

The corporate and public policy decisions that are made for inclusiveness will follow the flow of synchronicity and the universal laws of the land. Our reality of five hundred years ago is vastly different than that of today. What will be the average human frame of reference five hundred years from now? Will oneness of the individual, the community and the world be a natural way of existence? What is often not realized is that only through total integration of self can a coming together in the world occur. A rabbi by the name of David once said, "The Oneness we are is because of the differences we have."

   Individuality and connections vary among cultures. Until recently, the western view has placed much more emphasis on independence than most other cultures. The Nepalese, South Americans and other Third World countries place tremendous value on relationships. This value is the most important teaching the third world countries can share with those of us in the West who place greater importance on material accumulation and separateness. If we are not willing or able to learn from those who have a deeper appreciation and respect for connection, we may be in for a downfall far beyond the fate of the Roman Empire.

The universal lessons can be as tough as they come. We need only watch our television sets and hear commentators discuss citizens who have really pulled together to help the victims who have lost their homes due to the fire or flood or experienced a shattering earthquake. I smile when I hear well known individuals like Jerry Rice of the San Francisco 49ers say, "We played as a collective group and we win Super bowl games." (January 29, 1995).

We can live with adversity or we can learn to connect through spiritual harmony. In Webster's Dictionary, adversity has the same root as "satan."[2]   Our legal system is based on the adversarial model. This system must also change and become unified. Mediation is a primitive first step in resolving the separateness our legal system promotes. Connection within the legal community will eventually occur. It can be done easily or it can be done with difficulty. The choice is up to those in the legal community.

Division no longer works in our society. So the challenge is how do we keep our individual integrity while joining others in wholeness? One effort on my part is that before I speak, I will ask myself whether the words I speak will be separating or joining ones. I then choose to frame the comment so we can remain connected and still have truth expressed and heard. Separations also occur when I feel I have been injured by someone. My inability to forgive means I am wishing to change what happened to me in the past. I have no control over the past, and so forgiveness seems to be the most logical alternative.

It is difficult for me to believe that scientists or physicists will not listen to their inner voices in seeking the scientific answers to the projects they are working on. My feelings are as real as my thoughts; sometimes more so. I live with all my feelings and thoughts from moment to moment. I am no different than any other human including physicists.

Rachel Carson, the noted scientist who wrote **The Silent Spring**, combined scientific thought with societal and spiritual concerns. She proposed a holistic approach to a global problem. Scientists are now beginning to understand the greater need for harmony in the world today. Hopefully, our government leaders are learning the same. The cooperative principle is stronger than the competitive one **(Lifting the Veil, 1993).** Insects, animals, and vegetation are learning to live collectively together. Cross-fertilization between insects and plants exists and species provide transport for other organisms or their seeds. Science and spirituality have much in common, and through synchronicity these connections are becoming more apparent every moment.

The 70s was the "me" decade as we strive toward individuality. The decade of the 80s was the "we" experience. Reaching out and relating to significant others was the initial goal. The 90s, it seems, will be the "Thee" decade, which is defined according to the Quaker religion as "among friends". This will help in reaching a clearer connection with the universal life force. It is coming together through universal harmony.

Organized religions could show great courage and come together and putting aside their philosophical differences without losing their principles. For instance, the Koran (Radice, 1983) was revealed to the Prophet Mohammed by the Angel Gabriel. Angels are everywhere; they don't discriminate or separate. The **Koran** tells the story of Mary, and how the Angel was with her. The Christian religion has the same historical truth. Can they come together and put aside the semantics of believing in *only* one or the other in order to be "saved?" The real definition of sin is missing the mark or experiencing alienation by not connecting. Doesn't alienation occur when someone doesn't follow our religious beliefs? Our task is to choose to bring together all into the Light of wholeness without lessening the significance of each individual Light. As Marcial Boo' told me in Peru, *"there is no problem"*.

As we welcome the year 2000 into our lives we will realize our challenge is to work toward total integration of all things in our lives. It begins with One. The more we turn our back on this truth, the less harmony we will know and the greater the experience of pain and ultimate healing we will need. Pierre Teilhard de Chardin said,

> *"...a great hope held in common. The hope...a passionate longing to grow, to be, is what we need. Held in common...our hope can only be realized if it finds its expression in greater cohesion and greater human solidarity...we have the world in our souls."*

The law of synchronicity is the reality of our world. I feel universal connections when I am being guided by the inner voice that places me in a state of grace, or as I sit in my office interacting with a family in need, or see myself supporting a friend and smiling at a stranger, feeling the power of my presence and inner peace, or quietly taking in the wisdom of my grandchild. Living my life of ease is a new and welcomed path. I recognize the separateness of everyone and everything that allows me to ultimately treat everyone and everything the same in the Oneness of life. With the purity of this intention my path is clear and the angels are my companions. May the angels surround you with Love on your chosen path, and may all our paths come together in the Light.

[1]**In Search of the human language**, WGBH Television PBS Boston, Massachusetts, December 1994. Chris Hall, Producer.
[2]**Webster's New Collegiate Dictionary,** (1959) Second Edition, G. & C. Merriam Co. Publishers, Springfield, Mass. USA. Pg. 14

REFERENCES

ABBA, **I have a Dream** lyrics. Swedish composers Anderson and Ulvaeus (Sweden and Polar Music AB).

Anderson, Robert M., Jr., (1977). **A Holographic Model of Transpersonal Consciousness**. The Journal of Transpersonal Psychology, Vol. 9, No. 2, pp. 119-29.

Anonymous (1975). **A Course in Miracles**. Helen Schuoman remained anonymous. She channeled the writings while serving as a Professor at Columbia University. Foundation for Inner Peace, Tiburon, CA.

Beauman, Sally (February, 1988). **Destiny**, Bantam Books, NY.

Breslauer, S. Daniel, (Fall, 1976). **Abraham Maslow's Category of Peak-Experience and the Theological Critique of Religion**, Review of Religious Research, Vol. 18, (1) pp. 53-61.

Buhler, Charlotte, (Winter, 1979). **Humanistic Psychology as a Personal Experience**, J. Humanistic Psychology. V. 19, (1) pp. 5-21.

Carson, Rachel (1962), **Silent Spring**. See Linda Jean Shepherd, Ph.D. **Lifting the Veil**, p.2 of the reference section.

Daniel, A., Wyllie, T., Ramer, A., (1992). **Ask your Angels**. Ballantine Books, New York.

Darnton, John. (March 13, 1994). **English ordain women priests**. San Francisco Chronicle, pp. A-14.

Eadie, Betty (1992). **Embraced By the Light**. Gold Leaf Press, Placerville, CA.

Easwaran, Eknath, (1975). **The Bhagavad Gita for Daily Living**. Blue Mountain Center of Meditation, Berkeley, CA.

Fairbairn, W.R.D., (1954). **Psychoanalytic studies of the personality.** London: Travistock.

Ferguson, Marilyn (1980). **The Aquarian Conspiracy**, J.P. Tarcher, Los Angeles, CA.

Flinders, Carol Lee (1993). **Enduring Grace**, Harper, SF.

Fontana, David, (1993). **The Secret Language of Symbols**. Duncan Baird, London and Chronicle Books, San Francisco, CA. Publishers.

Guisinger, S., and Blatt, S.J. (February, 1994). **Individuality and relatedness - Evolution of a Fundamental Dialectic**. American Psychologist, pp. 104-11.

Heintzelman, Mark E., (1976). **Relationship between Religious Orthodoxy and Three Personality Variables**, Psychological Reports, Vol. 38, pp. 756-58.

His Holiness the Dalai Lama, 1975. **The Buddhism of Tibet**, Snow Lion Publications, New York.

Hood, Ralph W., Jr. (Spring, 1979). **Conceptual Criticisms of Regressive Explanations of Mysticism**, Review of Religious Research, Vol. 17, No. 3, pp. 179-87.

Hood, Ralph W., Jr. (1979). **Religious Orientation and the Report of Religious Experience**, Scientific Study of Religion, Vol. 9, No. 4, pp. 285-91.

Hood, Ralph W., Jr., (1977). **Differential Triggering of Mystical Experience as a Function of Self-actualization**, Review of Religious Research, Vol. 18, No. 3, pp. 264-70.

James W., (1902). **The Varieties of Religious Experience**, Collier, NY.

Jung, Carl, **The Collected Works of C.G. Jung**, (1971). A revision by R.F.C. Hull of the translation by H.G. Baynes, Princeton University Press.

Kornfield, Jack (1992). **Roots of Buddhist Psychology**. Dharma Seed Tape Library, Wendell Depot, Massachusetts.

Lemert, Charles, C., (Spring, 1975). **Defining Non-church Religion**, Review of Religious Research, Vol. 16 (3), pp. 186-97.

Maslow, Abraham, H. (1978). **Various Meanings for Transcendence**. J. of Transpersonal Psychology, V. 10 (2) pp. 56-66.

McPhee, Martha (March 6, 1994). **Tale of a Kathmandu shopping expedition**. San Francisco Chronicle, pp. T-3.

Moody, Raymond, (1976). **Life after Life**. Stackpole Books, Harrisburg, PA.

Moore, Molly (January 2, 1994). **Saving the Sherpa Life.** San Francisco Examiner and Washington Post. Mountain Travel-Sobek, 6420 Fairmount Avenue, El Cerrito, CA. 84530 Feature section.

Noyes, Russell (1978-79). **The Subjective Response to Life-threatening Danger**, Omega, Vol. 9 (4), pp. 313-21.

O'Rourke, Mary-Jo; Shrestha, Bimal (March, 1992). **Nepali phrasebook**. Lonely Planet Publications, Berkeley, CA.

Radice, Betty, Editor, (1983). **Koran**. Penguin Books, Middlesex, England.

Rinpoche, Sogyal (1992). **The Tibetan Book of Living and Dying**, Harper-San Francisco.

Schwartz, John (March 17, 1994). **World at a Loss for Words**, The San Francisco Chronicle, p. 3.

Segal, Erich (April, 1992). **Acts of Faith**, Bantam Books, NY.

Shepherd, Linda Jean, Ph.D. (1993). **Lifting the Veil**, Shamhala, Boston and London. (pp. 72, 231-33 reference to Rachel Carson, **Silent Spring**, (1962).

Spirit Rock Meditation Center (December 2, 1994), letter quotes M.K. Ghandi (sic).

Stace, W.T. (1960). **Mysticism and philosophy**, Lippencott, Philadelphia, PA.

Stanley, Gordon (1964). **Personality and Attitude Correlates of Religious Conversion**. Journal for the Scientific Study of Religion (4), pp. 60-63.

Stark, Rodney (1971). **Psychopathology and Religious Commitment**, Review of Religious Research, Vol. 12, pp. 165-76.

Sullivan, Pat (January 24, 1994). **Two Billion Dollar Hole in the Ground**. San Francisco Chronicle.

Teilhard, de Chardin. **The Phenomenon of Man**. Harper/Row, NY.

The Holy Bible, King James version (November, 1974). Penguin Group Publishers, NY, pp. 214-26.

The Treasure Candle, Inc., 5424 Fair Avenue, N. Hollywood, CA.

Websters' Dictionary (1959). New Collegiate, 2nd edition, G. & C. Merriam Co. Publishers, Springfield, Massachusetts, p. 14.

Welwood, John; Capra, Fritjof; Ferguson, Marilyn; Neeleman, Jacob; Pribram, Karl; Smith, Huston; Vaughan, Frances; Walsh, Roger N., (1978). **Psychology, Science and Spiritual Paths: Contemporary Issues**, Journal of Transpersonal Psychology, V 10, (2) pp. 93-111.

Wilde, Stuart (1987). **Life was never meant to be a struggle**. White Dove International, Taos, NM, pp. 1-49.

Paul + Carrol H.

THE EVEREST ESCAPADE

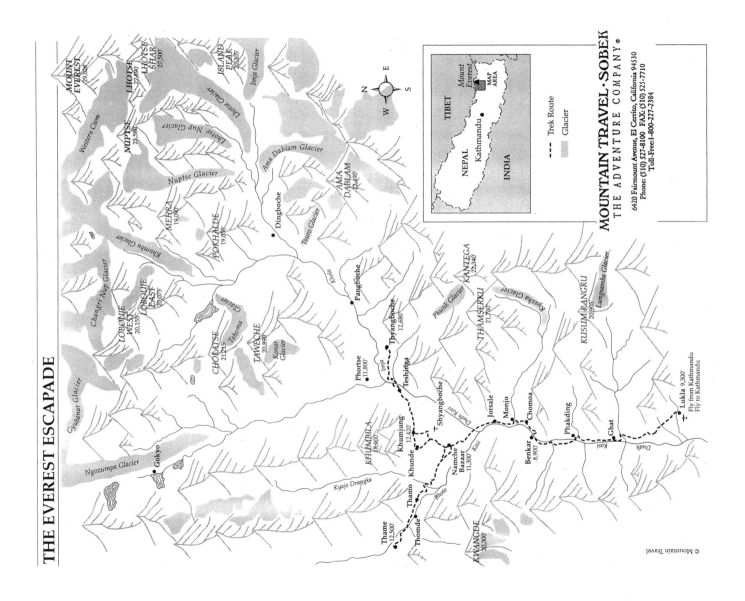

© Mountain Travel

MOUNTAIN TRAVEL · SOBEK
THE ADVENTURE COMPANY ⊕

6420 Fairmount Avenue, El Cerrito, California 94530
Phone: (510) 527-8100 FAX: (510) 525-7710
Toll-Free:1-800-227-2384

Trek Route
Glacier

COLOR LAB

May 20, 1994

Jerri Curry, Ph.D. MFCC
1530 Webster Street, Suite D
Fairfield, California 94533

Dear Dr. Curry:

Pursuant to your request to make two transparencies from the two negatives you provided our company, The ZIBA Color Labs, we encountered problems unexpected in the negative to positive conversion process. The standard exposure pack was no where near what was needed to generate the film positive. What seemed to be a dense negative was more problematic than we had ever experienced. The lens apperature was wide open at 5.6 and exposure was thirty seconds. The time of the exposure was more than twice what it would normally be in such a process.

The density of the negative does mean too much light was coming in to the camera at the time the picture was taken. It was far more problematic than we had experienced in the past.

Upon your return to our studio you told us about your experience in the Himalayas and that these two pictures were taken at that time. These two negatives as you call them "the Angel and the Circle of Light" are highly unusual negatives and we have no logical explanation for the process we had to go through to make the negative to positive conversion.

Sincerely yours,

Alex Katz, Assistant Manager

64 SHATTUCK SQ.
BERKELEY
CA 94704
415. 849. 0776